ROY BEAN

Judge Bean as he usually looked

C. L. SONNICHSEN

ROY BEAN

LAW WEST OF THE PECOS

THE DEVIN-ADAIR COMPANY
OLD GREENWICH, CONN.

OTHER BOOKS
BY
C. L. SONNICHSEN

Ten Texas Feuds
Alias Billy the Kid
I'll Die Before I'll Run
Cowboys and Cattle Kings
Billy King's Tombstone
The Mescaleros (*in preparation*)
Tularosa: The Story of the Great Feuds
    of Texas (*in preparation*)

  bcdefghijklmn
First published in MCMXLIII by the Macmillan Company
Manufactured in the United States of America
Library of Congress Catalog Number 58-9755

CONTENTS

ILLUSTRATIONS

PREFACE

When this book was first published in 1943, Roy Bean the self-styled Law West of the Pecos, had been dead for only forty years. Many people were still alive who knew the old rascal well—some who were present when he fined a corpse for carrying a concealed weapon and when he ruled that there was no law in the Texas statutes against killing a Chinaman. Pioneer times were just around the corner, too close to allow for very much romanticizing of such an unkempt, unscrupulous old four-flusher. Stuart Lake had begun the transformation of Wyatt Earp into something just a little lower than the more militant angels, and a Los Angeles newspaperman had declared in print that Billy the Kid had given his life "so that decent people might live." But Roy Bean! He was something else! What did *he* have to offer? He wasn't even a gunfighter—just the most notorious of all the frontier justices of the peace.

When it was suggested in the introductory chapter of this book that the American people were shopping for heroes and were looking Roy over to see if he would measure up to Robin Hood or Davy Crockett, reviewers snorted indignantly. Stanley Walker, writing for the New

York *Herald Tribune* (March 14, 1943), protested: "Crockett belongs to Valhalla; Bean was merely a tough, mean old rooster with a taste for trickery and low jokes." Hal Borland (*The New York Times*, April 11, 1943) agreed. Roy, he pointed out, "died of heart trouble in his own bed" (not the heroic way to go), and resembled nothing so much as "a haunch of billygoat meat. Very old goat at that."

Now thirty years more have gone by and Roy Bean is still with us. Clip-and-paste artisans periodically rewrite chapters from this book for the "true magazines." Two moving pictures have been made about Roy and his pen pal Lily Langtry (whom he never met), the second one (1972) starring Ava Gardner and Paul Newman. Davy Crockett has never rated this sort of attention.

The simple truth is that, as we move further from our frontier days, the Wyatt Earps and Buffalo Bills and Roy Beans become more and more interesting. They don't make them anymore. Each one could have existed only in his special time and place. We know that Earp was no such hero as Stuart Lake made him out to be; that Buffalo Bill was produced by the imaginations of several popular writers; that Roy Bean was an old fraud. But of such men our heroic legends must be made. They are what we have to work with, and we make the most of them. Bean's special contribution was a vein of frontier humor, gamy and crude but genuinely funny.

I have heard only one Bean story since the book was written, but it has the right flavor. It is about the time a lady of nonexistent virtue came to Langtry and in due course shot and killed a man who aroused her indignation. Roy Bean was called in as coroner and held an inquest. After very brief consideration, he rendered his verdict:

"This man committed suicide, and that's my rulin'."

A lawyer, who happened to be among the spectators, objected. "Roy, you can't hand down such a verdict. This man has obviously been murdered. You can't do it."

"Oh, yes, I can," Roy replied. "I told him if he played around with that chippy, he was committing suicide. And by God he did!"

What can you do with a man like that but enjoy him? And that is what we are doing.

C. L. Sonnichsen
El Paso, Texas
January 13, 1972

TO THE MEMORY

of the horse thieves, card sharps, drunks, killers, and desperadoes without whom there would have been no Law West of the Pecos

Men have forgotten how full clear and deep
The Yellowstone moved on the gravel and grass grew
When the land lay waiting for her westward people!

A. MacLeish, EMPIRE BUILDERS.

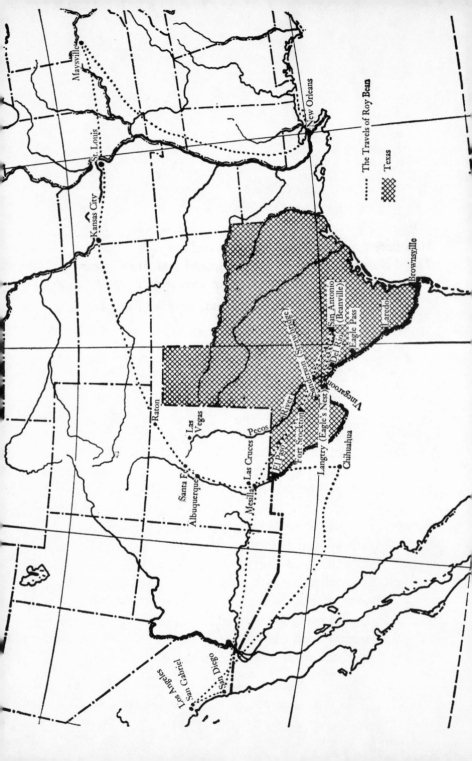

The Travels of Roy Bean ....
Texas ▨▨▨

MEET JUDGE BEAN

FIFTY YEARS AGO most of the male passengers on the Southern Pacific westbound from San Antonio to El Paso used to perk up a little as they approached the high bridge over the Pecos River. They knew that twenty miles beyond was a small oasis named Langtry where they would have fifteen or twenty minutes to stretch their legs, buy a drink, and pass the time of day with Judge Roy Bean.

Long before the coaches jarred to a halt in the shadow of the Langtry water tank, the greenhorns in the smoking car would have full information, some of it true, about the Law West of the Pecos, as Roy Bean called himself. With their curiosity already on edge they would take in the handful of adobe buildings which was Langtry, the little station and the big water tank, and finally the small frame shack twenty steps north of the tracks with a covered porch in front and signs plastered over it: THE JERSEY LILLY. JUDGE ROY BEAN NOTARY PUBLIC. LAW WEST OF THE PECOS.

Someone would say, "There he is!" And there he would be—a sturdy, gray-bearded figure with a Mexican sombrero on his head and a portly stomach mushrooming out over his belt, waiting on his porch for the swirl of business and excitement which always came at train time. You could see at a glance that he was as rough as a sand burr and tough as a boiled owl, but you realized also that he was a genuine character with plenty of salt in him.

If you came back more than once and really got to know

3

the old man, you found that he was a curious mixture of qualities. First you noticed that he was almost innocent of book learning, that he was egotistical and opinionated, that he regarded cheating you as good clean fun, and that he drank too much and washed too little. Once you got used to these drawbacks, however, you found that you had to like and even admire him. He was really a tough old rooster and had been a godsend to the ranger force when in 1882 they got him his commission as justice of the peace to help clean up the railroad construction camps. At the same time he concealed under his horny hide a heart which was not without soft spots. Children and animals liked him, and that is supposed to prove something. Then too, he was often generous in his own high-handed, tyrannical way. The poor Mexicans in the neighborhood would not have known what to do without his benevolent bullying. Finally, he had a color and flavor, authentic and attractive, which made people take an interest in him and forget about his profanity, unscrupulousness, and dirt.

The "best people," of course, have always been puzzled by a phenomenon like Roy Bean. Some of them still ask bitterly why such an old rapscallion should get so much attention when better men have lived and died unknown. The boys in the smoking car who piled off the train at Langtry and hot-footed it for the Jersey Lily never asked that question. They knew deep down among their instincts that Roy Bean, with all his faults and shortcomings—perhaps even because of them—was made out of the stuff of America. So they drank with him, played poker with him, laughed when he gypped them, and told epic tales about him which still go marching on.

They told about the time he held an inquest over a dead body on which he had found forty dollars and a pistol. He fined the corpse forty dollars for carrying concealed weapons.

They told about the Irishman who was brought into court for killing a Chinaman. Roy turned him loose, remarking that he had gone through his law book and found that it was homicide to kill a human being. "But," he said, "I'll be damned if I can find any place where it says it's against the law to kill a Chinaman."

They told about his habit of divorcing couples he had married, though he had no legal right to do so, explaining that he only "aimed to rectify his errors."

They told about his long-range platonic affair with Lily Langtry, the actress.

They told about the time he pulled off a heavyweight championship prize fight in his own back yard.

They told fifty yarns to show that he was too cagy to be taken in, too smart to be bluffed, and too tough to be damaged, and most of the stories were at least half true.

What they could not tell about, because they were not aware of it, was the real, deep-seated reason for Roy Bean's notoriety. They were not aware that the American people were examining old Roy as a candidate for hero worship—finding out if he could stand up to Davy Crockett and Mike Fink and Paul Bunyan; experimenting to see whether good folk stories could be made up about him; testing his quality to see if it was true frontier American.

This may seem like an eccentric and over-subtle way of looking at the old man, but there are arguments to justify it. No one doubts that older races than ours have been better able than we to evolve Robin Hoods, Siegfrieds, Rolands, and Arthurs to embody the national ideals. It is almost as plain to anyone who tries to understand our country that America has missed these symbols—has yearned for them

—has even gone out and kidnapped some likely prospects and made heroes of them by main force. Jesse James is one example. Billy the Kid is another. With the help of Hollywood we have constructed shrines for such drunken old tarts as Calamity Jane and have burned incense before such homicidal exhibitionists as Wild Bill Hickok. It looks as if the American People have gone shopping for heroes and come home with whatever they could find.

Perhaps we have to put up with so little because we have not wanted much. The fact is we demand less of our folk heroes than we do of our street sweepers and ditch diggers; the specifications for the type are almost shockingly simple. First of all we ask for a certain amount of ignorance. It makes our man seem more like one of us, and besides we have a dim superstition that too much education is destructive of horse sense. The real wise man, we think, is a child of nature. All he knows is what he reads in the papers; but he offers advice to kings and presidents just the same.

Early struggles and a background of poverty are a great help. It is even better if the candidate proves to be an orphan or if he ran away from home at an early age.

"Smartness" is necessary. Nobody wants to idealize a person who can be beaten in a horse trade.

Bravery—even pugnacity—is another essential. The only alternative is to be a master of the game of bluff. If a man we admire can fool his foes, we don't insist that he shoot them.

Most important of all, the aspirant to greatness must do things in a big way, even if he only lies in a big way about the things he does. If he can't rope a cyclone, use the new moon for a powder horn, or outrun a prairie fire, he has to be overwhelming in some other fashion—like calling himself the Law West of the Pecos and making it stick.

Most of the great Americans who have had enough vitality to start a run of legends about themselves have come close to this formula. If we take a liking to a strong personality who doesn't come close enough, we make him over almost before he is quiet in his grave. Even imaginary heroes like Pecos Bill and Paul Bunyan and Strap Buckner fit the pattern.

Roy Bean fits it too. He was not as big of bone as the great ones, but he belonged to the breed. And the most remarkable thing about him is the fact that he knew he belonged. Somehow he discovered that he was the kind of person Americans like to make something of, and he spent the last years of his life helping them make something of him. There were times when ambition burned low in him. His youth was full of color and adventure but he reached middle age without attracting much notice. When he began to crowd sixty, he was just another disreputable old tough living on the wrong side of town in San Antonio. There had been twenty years of this, and he was discouraged; but he never quite gave up the notion that he was a marked man. Then, at the beginning of the final quarter of his life, he went west with the railroad and found his place at last. In a few months he became the Law West of the Pecos, and a minor immortal.

Only one man in a million could have done it. His official residence was a one-room frame shack in which he held court, sold beer, slept, and cultivated his soul. His town was a hamlet of a few dozen inhabitants almost lost in the scorching wastes of the West Texas desert. His friends and acquaintances were cowboys and laborers and men on the dodge. What of it? He wanted to be the biggest man in the country and this was the sort of country in which he could be the biggest man.

For a while he lived the epic he imagined. He really was the Law in those parts for a few years. It was two hundred miles to the nearest justice court and naturally he had things his own way. Before long civilization and lawyers moved in on him, but by that time his saga was started and his position was assured. He became in the minds of other men a sort of Ulysses of West Texas—a man of craft and action combined—a figure of colorful peculiarities and great resourcefulness. His fame was no surprise to him, though it was to a great many other people, for he had been convinced all along that he was no ordinary citizen. He probably thought his recognition was, if anything, considerably overdue.

And so when the train pulled into Langtry, there he was on his porch. He always exposed himself at train time so people could see him. He was sure they would want to.

He knew also that he ought to have some sort of record ready for posterity. In his old tin trunk he kept a wad of clippings about himself which he always hoped would be helpful to his biographer. Once or twice he tried to get a wandering scribe to put it all down on paper, but somehow the job never got very far.

Naturally people misunderstood him. To many he was just an ignorant, crude, untidy old man with hardly enough moral sense to keep him out of jail—a hoary prevaricator who was entitled to perhaps a tenth of the notoriety he received. But to anyone willing to take a charitable view he was something more than this. He was a man trying to be the fundamental American, the essence of the era of expansion, the typical product of the frontier, the Pioneer with a big P.

Davy Crockett is his closest parallel, and Davy had the same feeling about himself. Like Roy, Davy thought he stood for something rugged and resistant in the life of the country. He took it for granted that he was somebody people ought to and did know about. And he never doubted that knowing him was an interesting and profitable experience.

It looks more and more as if Roy Bean succeeded in staking out a claim beside Crockett's in the minds of his countrymen. He has been fifty years in his grave but he isn't dead yet. The stories still go round. The articles still get written. The libraries still search out material for the curious every day. The State of Texas has landscaped and curried and smoothed his old Jersey Lily Saloon out of all recognition, and hundreds of tourists visit it every year as a sort of shrine. If he were still alive and you congratulated him to his face on becoming a folk hero, he would probably ask you what in hell you meant and might even fine you for contempt of court if he suspected you of having a dollar. Since he has settled down for a long nap in the Del Rio cemetery, however, it is probably safe to bring the matter up. At least it is high time for somebody to look into his history and see how a Roy Bean ever came to be at all.

ROY BEAN GROWS UP IN KENTUCKY WITH
SOME DIFFICULTY. HE HEADS SOUTHWEST
IN SEARCH OF ADVENTURE AND FINDS IT
WITH NO DIFFICULTY AT ALL.

There are some first rate men there, of the real half horse half alligator breed, with a sprinkling of the steamboat and such as grow nowhere on the face of the universal earth, but just about the backbone of North America.

THE AUTOBIOGRAPHY OF DAVY CROCKETT.

Strip away the shoddy romance that has covered up the real man and the figure that emerges is one familiar to every backwoods gathering, an assertive, opinionated, likable fellow, ready to fight, drink, dance, shoot or brag, the biggest frog in a very small puddle, first among the Smart Alecks of the canebrakes.

V. L. Parrington,
MAIN CURRENTS IN AMERICAN THOUGHT.

SPROUTING TIME

Judge Roy Bean never admitted publicly that he had ever been a child. The Law West of the Pecos was, or wished to be, a sage and serious figure. His tobacco-stained beard and bush of gray hair, his portly stomach drooping over his belt, his suspicious eye, his bull-of-the-woods voice—all fitted into the harmonious picture he took pleasure in presenting to the public. You might have thought he was created sixty-five years old, complete with beard and paunch, by direct action of an all-wise Providence.

He wasn't.

The fact is, Providence seems to have done its best to discourage him for the first two-thirds of his life. His struggles began between 1825 and 1830 in a cabin among the green hills of Mason County, Kentucky, along the Ohio River. His parents (whom he never mentioned) were named Francis and Anna Bean and they lived so humbly and obscurely that even the census-taker missed them. This was probably not the census-taker's fault. There is nothing on record to show that Francis and Anna Bean ever owned any property or had a permanent home anywhere. They were probably squatting off in the back woods somewhere and if census-taker Cleneay did blunder on their cabin in the spring of 1820, the whole family probably watched from the bushes at the edge of the clearing as he hammered in vain on their rough plank door.

They were so poor that Roy had an insatiable love of

money and display for the rest of his life. They were such
nobodies that he was willing to sacrifice anything for a little power and importance.

The contrast between himself and the other Beans in
Mason County didn't help Roy's feelings either. They were
a sturdy tribe, moderately well to do, and fond of gathering at the family homestead on Cabin Creek near Maysville to talk about their connections back in Maryland, the
exploits of their kinfolks in the Revolution and the War
of 1812, the days when they fought Simon Girty and the
Indians.

Roy was probably related to the Cabin Creek Beans (all
Beans are related), but he was a poor relation and had a
poor relation's pride in his family. In the good old Southern way he was always able to ignore his miserable circum-
stances and speak proudly of the clan. A Bean always did
thus and so, he would say, or a Bean wouldn't take this or
that off of anybody. This attitude played a part the time
his son Sam killed a man named Upshaw. Sam had got his
jaws slapped (for good cause) while his old man looked on.

"Goddam it, Sam!" roared his father. "Nobody ever
slapped a Bean and lived!"

And Sam picked up his old black powder rifle and shot
Upshaw dead.

Another time Roy noticed one of his small daughters
coming around the corner on a windy day. He pointed her
out to one of his friends, H. L. Howell.

"How's them for legs?" he inquired proudly. "All the
Beans got 'em."

In the immediate members of his family Roy found
some cause for pride. There were three boys known to history. Joshua was the oldest by several years. Sam (the only
one whose birth date is known) came along in 1819. Roy

was last. There is rumor also of a sister named Martha or Molly and a fourth brother, Jim. The boys were stocky, powerful fellows—ambitious, energetic, and determined. They were the kind of boys who would be comforting to have around in an Indian fight but who would be poor risks at a tea party. Any one of them could have been a Captain Kidd or a Commodore Vanderbilt or a Davy Crockett, and all three left a mark on their country. Josh had got to California at the time of the American occupation, and before he was murdered in 1852 he had become the first mayor of San Diego and a Major General of the State Militia. Sam was the first sheriff of Dona Ana County, New Mexico, when it reached nearly to the Pacific Ocean. Roy never was more than a justice of the peace in an almost imperceptible town in West Texas, but he came closest of all to being a Great Man.

Culture and background being out of his reach, young Roy picked up the usual frontier education. He became familiar with guns and animals and learned to make a swap to his own advantage. He grew used to getting along on not very much. He could turn his hand to anything from courting a girl to butchering a hog. He learned to fight and to drink whiskey and to think of moving farther west to make his fortune.

If he had more than three months in the log schoolhouse he was lucky, for education wasn't so easy to get in those days. He learned to read a little and to write less. To the end of his days he signed his name laboriously and got somebody else to write his letters whenever he could. His son Sam, who absorbed a fair amount of schooling, handled all the family correspondence as soon as he was able. Ignorant as he was, Roy liked to have people think he was fond of reading, and kept his place cluttered up with newspapers and magazines; but a good many saw through him anyhow. They noticed that when he stood up to perform a marriage ceremony or other official act, he turned the pages of his book too fast to be reading the words he repeated.

They even said (behind his back) that he was *illiterate*. It made Roy boil.

He boiled over once in the early nineties when a friend of his, Myron W. Tracy, sent off a story using the horrid word to one of the Chicago papers. Roy sharpened a pencil stub, sweated out an angry letter of protest, and got Mr. True, then agent at the Langtry station, to witness that it was written by Roy Bean and no other. Muttering awful things, he mailed the letter which Tracy received in due time.

Like most boys who got their education with an axe and a rifle, Roy saw no need for prolonging his school days. It was in his blood to move on, to keep ahead of the restraints of law and order. Besides, everybody else was doing it. Josh left for California. Sam went around with a far-away look in his eye and finally pulled out too. Roy was the only one left.

In those days a favorite adventure for boys from Kentucky and Tennessee was to take a raft of logs or a flatboat loaded with lard and whiskey and tobacco down to New Orleans. When he was "about sixteen," Roy sometimes hinted, he made the New Orleans trip himself. He went with a party taking a batch of slaves to market. The negroes were worth more in New Orleans than in Kentucky. It was a good trip, but it had the usual ending for Roy Bean. He set out to see the sights and somewhere, somehow, he ran into trouble. With all speed he took out for home—and that was another episode he wouldn't talk about.

It is possible that he drifted farther than New Orleans on this or a later expedition. He was once heard to say that he had driven an ammunition wagon for General Taylor's army in the Mexican War and had met Lee, Grant, Kearney, and others who later became famous. Maybe he did, but if so he carefully concealed his tracks.

A few other bits of driftwood from his lost youth sometimes came to the top. They seldom came up twice in the same form, but they were good stories anyway. His favorite was probably the one about his strangest meal. Sometimes he set the tale in Canada. Sometimes it happened when he was hauling freight to California (which he never did). It seems that he was the junior member of an expedition of some sort which got lost and ran out of food far from civilization. It was cold and the ground was covered with snow. They rode for days. They killed their horses and ate them. Then they walked for days. Finally the captain said, "Boys, I'll get up early in the morning and see if I can kill some game. I'll take old Sam with me. You trail me up when it comes daylight." In the morning he and the negro Sam were gone.

They trailed him all day, and at night they saw his camp fire. Half a mile away they smelled meat cooking so they hurried in and were soon eating for the first time in many days. It was good-tasting meat. They wondered why old Sam wasn't there to share it.

"He's down to the river for water," said the captain.

Roy was fond of the old darky and began to worry when an hour went by and no Sam appeared. Carelessly, as if going for a stroll, he wandered down to the river. There he came upon some entrails and pieces of black skin hidden in the bushes.

Back at camp he questioned the captain: "What's become of Sam?"

"If you ask me that question again," said the man grimly, "I'll shoot you right between the eyes."

"I felt mighty bad about it"—Roy would say, taking his cigar out of his mouth—"mighty bad. Old Sam sure was good to me and took the best care of me he could, but I guess I ate a piece of him. I suppose I'll go to hell for it."

It didn't do any good to pump him for further details. He didn't want people to know about his sprouting time and if they were too curious he intentionally misled them. On his own say-so he was a Missourian, an Illinoisan, a Kentuckian. Lily Langtry was sure he was a Canadian. He even spread a report that his real name was Roy Boone and that he was a close relative of the great and original Daniel.

In other words the Roy Bean myth has had considerable help from Roy Bean.

SOUTHWESTWARD HO!

IN THE SUMMER of 1847 Sam Bean came home and sat his weary bones down on the doorstep as if he never wanted to move. He was lean and hard, and his skin was a rich walnut shade where it showed through his bushy beard.

"Where you been, Sam?" they asked him.

"Fightin' the Mexicans," said Sam. "I just got my discharge at New Orleans the end of June and I ain't fixin' to fight any more wars."

In the days that followed they heard all about it—all about the great plains and the high mountains, the strange men and the lovely women, the fighting and suffering and adventure.

It would be something to hear those stories that Sam told on the shady side of the house that summer while the younger Beans' mouths hung open and their eyes popped. Well, strangely enough it is still possible to hear them. Four months before he died in 1903 Sam wrote some of his memories down and gave them to a local newspaper. This is Sam's account, touched up by the editor of the *Rio Grande Republican*, Las Cruces, New Mexico:

"I left Kentucky near Louisville in the year 1845, and came to Independence, Mo. That was a fast town in those days; the tide of emigration had set in for Oregon; the town was alive with emigrants, and being headquarters for the Santa Fe and Chihuahua traders, the teamsters also who were always there in force formed a considerable portion

of the surging throng destined to cross the great American
deserts. Everybody seemed imbued with the spirit of adventure. I was young then, and in for anything that was
tinged with romance or wild adventure, and nothing
thrilled my nerves so much as the stories the teamsters
would tell us in Independence where a large number were
congregated to hire their services as veterans of the plains,
to steer a ten-mule wagon and team or six yoke of oxen
across that desert of a thousand miles, fraught with danger
at every step. There was a regular place of meeting of the
teamsters every night, and all the young bloods of the
neighborhood who were anxious to make the plunge into
the great wilds of the West would be there. They would
tell about the buffalo hunts and blood curdling stories
about the frequent battles with the Comanche and Arapaho
Indians. The hardships of the voyage and what they suffered they knew would not be so interesting to the boys,
and that phase of the trip was purposely kept in the background. To cap the climax, they would wind up with a
graphic description of the dark-eyed Señoritas in the land
of the Montezumas; that was a clincher, and all the waver-
ing fell into line, determined to go to the Spanish country,
as New Mexico was then called. I caught the prevailing
fever, too, and without any necessity for so doing went
and hired to drive a team of six yoke of oxen and a wagon
to Santa Fe, in the month of May, 1845. To walk a thousand miles across a forlorn desert, in those times, that was
the ultra test of manhood; and the boy or man who could
do that was considered a manly man. Others had done it,
why could not I do the same? One novel attraction in
Independence, at times, was the merchant's return trains
from Chihuahua dumping down in the streets thousands
and thousands of silver Mexican dollars, then at a par with

American gold all over the United States. The dollars were sewed up in green rawhide bags which when dry were as hard as boulders, that being found to be the safest way of transporting the money from Mexico. The starting and getting the wagons out on the prairies was a very perplexing business. Wild oxen and mules caught up on the prairies had to be harnessed and assigned to the wagons; for the first time they felt the manilla rope on their necks. But the Missouri boys of muscle and brawn knew how to manage the wild mules and oxen, some of them as wild and ferocious as if they had come from the jungles of Africa. Think of the poor drivers who had to pick out the mates and yoke them up every morning for the day's journey over swollen creeks and small rivers, that came up to the armpits and left the water sloshing in the shoes. Often have I slept of a night with wet feet and body wet up to my arms, but never took cold. There was a very strange infatuation about these men; they would go trip after trip across the plains, and the oftener they went and the more hardships they suffered the more intense was the desire to go again. They became veterans of the plains and veteran teamsters; robust wiry young fellows, they never were so happy in their lives as when they were popping their whips over their teams way out in the buffalo part of the desert, where the Comanche Indians were watching their every movement. Whenever the moon shone bright, the train of two hundred wagons was traveling until the moon waned. In the stillness of the night they would ring the changes on their old Missouri songs, and when on the return voyage, homeward bound, as they left Mexico behind them they had a beautiful farewell song they would sing. I only remember the beginning: it ran thus, 'Farewell, ye green fields and meadows, adieu;

ye rocks and ye mountains, I hasten from yóu.' There were eight of us, all young Missouri boys, who formed a party to come back to 'God's country,' as we used to call it, and we had a hard time of it, with some eventful scenes. Our provisions for the road consisted of hard bread and dried beef, and we bought mules at Santa Fe to ride home. On the Cimarron River we were overtaken by a fearful storm. One whole night, which seemed to be a month long, we sat all in a row with wet blankets frozen to us. There was not enough wood within fifty miles of the place to make a tooth-pick of; the buffalo chips were saturated with water, and we were in a fearful condition; but that long night with its horrors had an ending, and the boys shouted 'Glory to God' as the sun come out in great splendor in the morning. We had passed a fearful ordeal, and suffered intensely the whole night. The sun warmed us up, dried our clothes and blankets, and we began to feel like we would once more tread Missouri soil and see our friends. We were all young and without experience, having never been from home before and never beyond the sight of houses or beyond the pale of civilization. After getting in good shape again we resumed our travels, thinking about home and longing to see the smoke as it 'so gracefully curled' from the happy cabins in Missouri.

"Another disaster was in store for us, however, and it was unexpected. We had not noticed that our provisions were nearly exhausted, and we were yet five hundred miles from the white settlements, which meant 'Home, sweet home,' with all its endearments—among kindred and friends. We traveled on for about one hundred miles further, when, like a clap of thunder, the fact stared us in the face that our provisions were gone. We found ourselves now in a predicament; still four hundred miles from home, we were crossing what are now the great states of Colorado and Kansas, then without a solitary house or inhabitant in all that area of wild country, claimed by the Indians as their exclusive domain. To all appearances it seemed that we were doomed, and that death by starvation would be our ultimate fate; and that, as we shuffled off this mortal coil one at a time, the survivors would not have strength enough to bury the dead, and our bones would be left to bleach on the desert plains. With all this dire distress hanging over us, we still had a lingering hope that something would turn up for our deliverance. And sure enough, after being three days and nights without food we discovered fresh wagon tracks coming into the Santa Fe road going towards Missouri. Our salvation depended on making haste to overtake that train. The train was traveling at a rapid rate for the purpose of out-traveling the Indians, and was composed of all the rich Armijo merchants of New Mexico. They had a large bulk of money in their wagons, ten of which were loaded with fresh buffalo meat they had killed, for their party to live on. After pushing on with all possible speed, we saw by the light of the moon about ten o'clock at night the sheets of the wagons far in the distance and a shout went up from our little party. On nearing the camp of the Mexicans about forty armed men came out to interview us and see who we were. We told them who we were and they invited us into their camp, and gave us an abundance of buffalo meat for the next fifteen days, until we reached Independence, all in good health and spirits. The news of our eventful trip had traveled faster than we did, and the reporters were already to hear the story of our sufferings and hardships on the great desert. Whilst the memory of these were yet fresh in mind, I made a promise that I would never go across that fearful desert again, or beyond the confines of civilization; but it only took a few months for that feeling to wear off, and when spring opened war with Mexico broke out, and I enlisted as a twelve-months' volunteer soldier, to traverse not only the same but other deserts, and endure more hardships in a much longer voyage. I thought all the spirit of romance and adventure had been knocked out of me by my war experience, and that I would forevermore be content to remain within the lines of peace and civilization; but as soon as I received my discharge from the army my brain was busy laying plans again for another trip across the plains. I come out with my brother, went on a trading expedition to Chihuahua, and this was my third trip across the great American desert, now covered by the rich state of Colorado.

"SAMUEL G. BEAN."

Sam's last sentence explains how brother Roy came to leave home for good—he went west as junior partner in the unincorporated firm of Bean and Bean, Santa Fe traders. They got to Independence in the spring of 1848, picked up mules and wagon, and spent what money they had (it probably wasn't much) on a stock of goods for trading. Then they joined a wagon train, snailed across the plains to Santa Fe, decided there was more money farther on, and finally pitched camp at Chihuahua, Mexico. Chihuahua was hungry for American goods and kind to strangers. In a short time the brothers had a small trading post going where they sold everything they could get hold of for which there was a demand—including whiskey. Meanwhile they enjoyed themselves. Americans were not too common in those parts, and for the first time in his life Roy knew the satisfaction of feeling different and slightly superior. The natives translated his name and called him and Sam "Los Frijoles," to Roy's amusement. He learned a little Spanish and began to live in the Mexican way—leisurely with proper attention to his rest and his pleasures. He went to cock fights. He drank tequila. He investigated the attractions of the Mexican women who fell in his way. He learned to love chile, especially chile con carne made with liver. Kentucky, he thought, was never like this.

In Roy Bean's life, however, good things never seemed to last. Just when he was beginning to feel permanent somewhere, there would be an explosion and out he would go. The eruption in Chihuahua was the first of a long series of hasty exits and it must have been a very colorful affair for he wouldn't talk about it. All his friends in later years knew vaguely that he had got into trouble in Mexico in his youth but that was as far as their knowledge went. The only man he confided in was apparently a young California immigrant, Horace Bell, who became his friend while they both were living in the neighborhood of Los Angeles. Fortunately Horace Bell (who afterward acquired the title of Major) remembered most of what he heard when he began to write books many years later.

It seems that trouble and whiskey as usual went together. One day a big Mexican badman got lit up and took it into his head to clean out the gringos. He began on Roy and dropped dead with a bullet between his eyes after an exchange of shots. In the eyes of the Americans it was a fair fight; in the eyes of the Mexicans it was murder.

Bare feet pattered through the town. The news spread and little knots of muttering people began to clot into a mob. Somebody made a speech and worked himself up into a demand for blood. They closed in on the Bean *tienda* just after a couple of wagons slipped out of Chihuahua carrying all the American traders in town with their most valuable and portable goods. The Bean wagon was well out in the lead.

They stopped a good distance away at the mining town of Jesus Maria in northern Sonora, but news of their coming got there ahead of them and a reception committee was already being organized.

"A conflict ensued," says Major Bell, "with the final result that the Americans in Jesus Maria were driven out. Their stores were sacked and they barely escaped with their lives. They finally found refuge in California after a terrible journey."

Sam didn't go along. He was interested in a Chihuahua girl named Petra Kirker whose father had been selling Apache scalps to the Mexican government until the government began to suspect that the similarity between Mexican and Indian hair was making Mr. Kirker too much money. Petra was sixteen years old when Sam married her in Juarez in March, 1849. There might be a story there if anybody were left to tell it.

As for Roy, he always said that he came out to California with the gold rush. As far as dates go, he was a forty-niner all right; but when he joined the rush, he was undoubtedly impelled by a metal much baser than gold.

DUEL IN SAN DIEGO

Roy PULLED UP his weary horse and saluted the Mexican in the lumbering, wooden-wheeled cart.

"*Buenas tardes, Señor*," said the Mexican, politely removing his corn-shuck cigarette from his mouth.

"Do you know," inquired Roy in his best Spanish, "an American named Bean who lives here?"

"Bean? *Seguro que sí!* Everybody knows him. He is the *alcálde*."

Alcálde! That was something between a mayor, a police judge, and a Lord High Executioner. Sometimes there would be two or three of them in a single town, but always the top *alcálde* ran the civil affairs of the pueblo. Roy guessed that Josh would be the *alcálde mayór*, if there was more than one.

"*Mil gracias, amigo*," he said to the Mexican and rode on into the little Spanish pueblo of San Diego, whose adobe walls and tile roofs were just ahead with the old presidio rising up in the midst.

Josh was glad to see Roy but not as glad as Roy was to see Josh. Danger and starvation and poverty were far behind now and happy days were at hand, for Joshua Bean was not just a Yankee trader with a finger in local politics; he was a power in the affairs of the whole region, and to be his brother was to be Somebody.

It would be a good thing to know more about Josh, but he was too much of a Bean to be easily traced. He came

out with the American soldiers in 1846, and Major Bell
says he was a captain in the regular army during the Mexican War; but his name is unknown to the War Department. Like his brothers he seems to have been a hard-
hitting frontier character who liked Mexican women and
straight whiskey. In a time of change and danger he was
a pretty useful fellow and became very popular with both
Mexicans and Americans in San Diego. He had influence
(and money) enough to become *alcálde* just before Roy
arrived, and in 1850, when American forms of local government began to be used, he became San Diego's first
mayor. About that time the Territorial Legislature was
organized, and in the spring of 1850 Josh was officially
appointed Major General of the State Militia. Thence-
forward he was happy to be known as General Bean. His
Spanish speaking friends called him "General Frijol."

Nothing could have suited Roy better than to shine in
the reflected splendor of the General. The best homes in
San Diego were open to him and all the pleasures of a
Spanish town were at his service. There is little reason
for supposing that he spent much time among the refinements of the best homes, but in the cock-fighting, tippling,
carefree society of the *pulperías* he soon became a leader.
How he enjoyed it! Fandangos, horse racing, gambling,
love in the moonlight—all for the brother of General
Frijol! Kentucky? Where was Kentucky, anyhow? Roy
wondered sometimes if he had ever been there.

You would hardly have recognized him as the raw
backwoods boy of two years before. He had filled out and
toughened (if that was possible) in those months of ad-
venturous life. He spoke reasonably good Spanish and
tickled himself tremendously by adopting Spanish manners and acting the Mexican gentleman.

"He was quite a dashing figure of a young buck and was soon prancing around the old town appareled in all the gay trappings of a California caballero on a spirited steed with silver-mounted saddle and bridle, and became the beau ideal of the aristocratic señoritas of California's original white man's settlement. . . . Those warm-hearted little California beauties just went wild over the handsome fellow; for, as a matter of fact, Roy Bean was as handsome as an Adonis. His complexion was as fair and rosy as a girl's. Hair black and silky, figure above medium height and perfect. In manners a Chesterfieldian gallant."

This is Major Bell's notion of how Roy looked after a few months in the congenial air of San Diego. No doubt the picture is colored up a bit, and it certainly does not look much like old Roy Bean of Langtry, Texas; but every Bean has his day and this was Roy's.

He was so busy being gay in the Spanish fashion that he decided to stay when Josh pulled up stakes early in 1851 and moved north where there was more going on. It may be that he was left to take care of the odds and ends of business affairs which were left dangling when Josh went to San Gabriel, but the chances are Roy was just having too much fun to move.

Very shortly, however, he did move—very fast, and not because he wanted to.

There happened to be a Scotchman named Collins in town, who was vain and boastful of his pistol shooting. Roy was vain and boastful of his pistol shooting, too. One day they engaged in a bragging contest about it, and Collins said he thought it would be a good idea if they had a shooting match.

"Sure," said Roy. "How do you want to shoot, and what at?"

"Let's fire at a target from a moving horse."

"Walk, trot, or gallop?"

"Make it a gallop."

"All right. I'm agreeable."

"What shall we use for a target?"

Roy's serpent eye gleamed maliciously. "I suggest," he said, "that you shoot at me and I shoot at you."

Mr. Collins was rudely shocked by this proposal, but he had started it all and he couldn't stop now.

"All right," he agreed weakly.

As news of the duel spread, San Diego became wildly excited and chattered of nothing else. There was a fine old Spanish custom in operation at the time which encouraged duelling on horseback with swords or lances—but pistols! That was really serious! It was better than a bull fight!

When the authorities got wind of the affair they asked themselves if this thing could really be in a civilized community and, if so, what a peace officer was supposed to do about it. As they thought it over it seemed more than probable that one or other of the principals would weaken and turn up missing before the fighting began. Besides, the merchants were expecting to fill their cash boxes if a crowd turned out, and they objected vigorously to any suggestion of stopping the duel. So Sheriff Agostin Haraszthy merely cautioned Bean and Collins that if and when the shooting started it must be in a direction away from spectators.

The nerve of both men was equal to the test and they appeared at the time set—it was on February 24, 1852—on horseback and armed with pistols.

A huge crowd was out to see the blood and fun, and that made things difficult. The main street of the town was used as a duelling ground, and since both sides were lined with people, it was hard to shoot without knocking over a few spectators. Back and forth and round and round the duellists galloped, jockeying for position. Finally Roy cut loose, winged Collins, and then shot his horse out from under him. Man and horse went down in a heap in the middle of the street. About that time Sheriff Haraszthy decided that matters had gone too far and arrested both pistoleers.

The editor of the San Diego *Herald* took notice of the fray in his next issue.

Shooting affair—Mr. Roy Bean was held to bail on last Tuesday, for shooting a man, whose name we did not learn. The wound is in the leg, and he was shot while on his horse, and in the act of escaping from Bean, who had a moment previous snapped the pistol at his head. Private difficulty was the cause.

For a month Roy endured confinement in the San Diego jail before the leisurely process of California law got around to giving him a hearing. Judge Ames then bound him and Collins over for a thousand dollars each to appear at the next term of court. Both were charged with assault with intent to murder; Collins was also accused of challenging to fight a duel, and Roy of accepting a challenge to fight a duel. Burdened with these accusations they went back to their cells.

According to Major Bell this was no hardship for Roy. The Mexican girls of the Old Town "stormed the jail with baskets and shawls filled with flowers, cold chicken, tamales, enchiladas, dulces, wines and cigars, and crowded for position at the gratings to hand their gifts through to their Adonis."

This lasted for a month more. Then Roy began to feel

bored even with the señoritas who "stormed" the *juzgado*. Could the jail be cracked, he wondered.

At first thought there seemed no possibility of a break, for the building was new and the particular pride of Sheriff Haraszthy, who had supervised the construction. It was made of cobblestones set in an unheard-of material called concrete, and half of San Diego swore proudly that it was as safe as the United States Treasury. The other half had its doubts. Roy settled the debate by engaging in a trial of strength with the jail in which the jail lost.

He needed outside help to do it, however.

"No jail could hold a hero whom so many beautiful women were passionately determined should be freed," says Major Bell. With tools provided by his admiring female friends Roy dug his way out through the walls of his cell. Later he said no tools were needed to dig out of a public contract job like that.

San Diego antiquaries doubt that Roy was the one who dug his way out of their jail. They say it was half a dozen drunken Indians, and they didn't dig their way out; they went out through a window on March 6, 1852. The antiquaries admit, nevertheless, that there are irrepressible legends about somebody digging out of that wonderful jail.

The *Herald*, dead to romance, merely noted on April 17 that Roy Bean "broke jail and escaped" several days before and that Collins was acquitted when he came up for trial.

Let Major Bell have the last word: "True gallant that he was, he afterward denied that the ladies supplied him with contraband. . . . However some one had seen to it that his horse stood all caparisoned behind the jail, with holster and pistol swung at the pommel, and the young gentleman cut stick for Los Angeles."

THE HEADQUARTERS SALOON

Los Angeles in those days was about the toughest place on the Pacific coast, if not in the world. It was close enough to Mexican soil to offer a refuge to any American desperado who needed one and at the same time it was within reach of any Mexican *ladrón* who was in demand south of the border. The scum of the Eastern states and territories gathered there to mingle with the homebred variety, to gamble, drink, and fight. Great bandits like Murietta hung around in perfect safety, preying on the land and enjoying the protection and admiration of high and low. About the time Roy arrived, a vigilante force was being organized.

In the middle of it all Roy Bean found his brother the General. He was in business at the old mission village of San Gabriel, nine miles from Los Angeles, and his Headquarters Saloon was the largest and most pretentious of the three in the village. It was at the southwest corner of the mission building inside which the General had his living quarters, and its whitewashed front presented a remarkably spotless appearance, considering that it was owned by one of the Bean boys. Business was very good, especially on Sundays when Josh put on horse races and cock fights for the public. On the Holy Sabbath and on fiesta days great crowds of large and small badmen jostled respectable citizens on their way to the bar. Fights were common and blood flowed as freely, though perhaps not as often, as whiskey.

For the second time Josh found a place for his brother.

As one Bean to another he welcomed Roy, found a place for him to sleep, and put him to work.

Of course with Roy "work" was a relative term. Physical labor was something he had only a speaking acquaintance with, but he would put out considerable effort to get something for nothing, to get talked about, or to get happy with joyful companions. The Headquarters Saloon was the sort of place to call forth his best efforts and he took to the bartender's apron and bungstarter as David did to a slingshot. From that period of his life on, Roy Bean was never content unless he could get behind a bar.

It was in April, 1852, that he began playing a spirited second fiddle to Josh at San Gabriel. In November of that year he was promoted to first violin, Josh being transferred to the harp section.

The assassination of General Bean is a famous episode in early California history and has been carefully examined in several books, not so much because of the importance of the General himself as because of his opposition. The murder was probably planned by the great Joaquin Murietta.

There was a woman in it, of course. Some say she was Joaquin's own *querida*. Others (including Major Bell) believe that she belonged to Joaquin's right-hand man, Felipe Read. The important point is that Josh was very much a Bean in his gallantry and was shot very dead as a result.

It happened about eleven o'clock of a Sunday evening. The day had been a lively one—Sundays always were at the Headquarters—and the final treat was a performance of the *Maromas*, a sort of Mexican circus. About eleven o'clock the General applauded the last performer, got his horse, and started home.

As he approached the Mission two shots were fired at him from the darkness, one taking him in the breast and passing entirely through his body. He fell from his horse, but as he fell he drew his pistol and fired three times from the ground at his attackers. He hit nobody.

Gathering his strength, he staggered to Juan Rico's house which was near by. In the morning he died.

A poor Mexican cobbler, Cipriano Sandoval, was accused of the killing, and it was made to appear that he was taking revenge for Bean's attentions to an Indian girl who had become interesting to both of them. With two others Cipriano was railroaded to the gallows, but the wise ones felt then, and still feel, that Murietta was behind it all.

Anyway, it was the beginning of the end for Murietta. Posses were organized at once to run his band to earth. Major Bell says Roy served with him as a ranger on one of these expeditions, but his name does not appear on the rosters of any of the formally organized companies. Being a Bean, he probably wanted no strings on him and just went along when he felt like it. He was certainly not a member of the company under Ranger Harry Love which brought back Joaquin's head (or what some people thought was Joaquin's head)—the head which was preserved in alcohol in a San Francisco saloon until 1906 when the fire and earthquake destroyed it along with other precious relics.

There is probably a good deal of unrecorded backstage history concerning this affair. Major Bell wrote the story up as fiction one time, privately declaring that his tale was really "history dressed up as romance." The unpublished manuscript, now in possession of Major Bell's editor, Lanier Bartlett, describes a battle in which Mexican bandits, disguised as California revolutionists, are besieging Roy and some other Americans in the Headquarters Saloon. Josh is in Los Angeles. Hearing of the assault, he rides to the rescue but is killed by the bandits before Hope's rangers can raise the siege. Roy is seriously wounded. "There is a beautiful native mestiza girl," says Mr. Bartlett, "who plays a thrilling part as the sweetheart of Joshua."

Whatever the facts were behind Joshua's taking off, the new situation had its points as far as Roy was concerned. As Joshua's next of kin he naturally took over the property and thus became the sole owner of the popular and thriving Headquarters. It was the summit of his worldly achievement in some ways. Never again was he to enjoy such a perfect combination of money, influence, pleasure, and youth. He had a two-hundred-dollar saddle and a fifty-dollar hat. He dressed in Mexican costume with sombrero, sash, embroidered pants, and red-topped boots. In one boot he carried a knife, while a pair of navy revolvers decorated his belt. With his black beard, arrogant eye, and game-cock carriage he had no trouble convincing most people that he was somebody important.

Major Bell, who thus describes him, met him in the spring of 1853 when he rode out to San Gabriel on business. Roy was at the door of the Headquarters, a "handsome, black-bearded young man." Bell asked him if he could get barley for his horse.

" 'Yes,' said he, 'as soon as Vicente comes in.'

" 'When will Vicente come in?' I inquired.

" 'When they get through hanging that fellow,' said he.

" 'What fellow?' said I.

" 'Oh!' said he, 'the Injuns have begun to learn the white man's tricks. By——' said he with a laugh, 'look! Isn't that rich?'

"While thus conversing my attention was drawn some 200 yards to the west, to a large crowd of Mexicans and Indians, men, women, and children, on foot and on horseback, and when Roy laughed and said 'Isn't that rich?' I saw a man go directly upward to the limb of a tree and there remain until an hour later, when, with a feeling in strange contrast with the exhilaration felt on approaching the pleasant-looking place, I took my departure without getting the feed of barley for my gallant little charger. After crossing the arroyo, and being about a half-mile away, I halted, turned my horse's head, and there still hung the poor victim dangling in the air. At the same time there went up a wail of despair as though from the friends and relatives of the murdered Indian. When Roy said, 'Isn't that rich?' he concluded with: 'Watch my front door and see that no d——d thief steals my whiskey,' and without another word hastily mounted his horse and dashed off to the place of execution, evidently intent on more readily drinking in the rapture of the occasion."

That unpromising beginning led to a friendship between Messrs. Bell and Bean which lasted for many years—long after Roy had left California. The Major was often present at the Headquarters when Roy, "in all the pomp and glory of being the cock of the walk, walked up and down, in and around, bucking here and there, and offering to bet on his favorite cock, making a cow for the horse race, dressed in his usual Mexican costume." He describes one notable happening which took place at Roy's establishment in December of 1854.

It was a Sunday afternoon and the place was jammed with roughnecks and desperadoes. Out back, a cock fight and a Mexican circus were whooping it up. In front, there was bawling and sweating as a horse race got started. Inside the saloon two monte games added spice to the drinking and carousing. The big room was loud with alcoholic talk and laughter, hazy with cigar smoke, reeking with whiskey fumes.

In at the door slid a little man with a pale face and

stylish clothes. He looked so completely out of place in that den of cutthroats that everybody noticed him. Modestly he made his way to the bar and ordered some refreshment.

Among those present was a very large, very bad man who figured he was about as tough as they came and who frequently described himself as "the bloodiest man in the Cherokee nation." It seemed to him that this was a good chance for a little humorous byplay, so he swaggered over to the little man, announced himself loudly, and shouted, "I'm going to kill you if you just open your mouth!"

Roy saw the beginning of trouble and shouldered his way up.

"Here," he said, "stop it! This boy is patronizing my bar and I'll protect him."

The little man now spoke up for himself. "I thank you," he said politely to Roy, "but the gentleman is not dangerous, in my opinion, and won't hurt anybody."

Then he whipped out a small pistol with one hand and held the bully up, while with the other he lit a cigar. When the stogie was going, he made his man stand still while he shoved the burning end up his nose.

It turned out that the little fellow was Joe Stokes, a brother of the man who later shot railroad magnate Jim Fisk.

"Little Joe Stokes was the Napoleon of the San Gabriel Headquarters," says Major Bell, "until a late hour of the day when he and myself rode into Los Angeles."

Major Bell's picture is the last we get of Roy at the crest of his early career. The next time he appears is at the establishment of his brother Sam at Mesilla, New Mexico, four or five years later with all signs of prosperity gone. No red-topped boots now; no silver-hilted bowie knife— he was a derelict with hardly enough clothes for decency.

What had happened?

Well, for one thing his luck had changed as did that of hundreds of other Californians. About the time Joe Stokes put on his act at the Headquarters the boom began to play out in California and there were many bankruptcies. Roy was shrewd but he was no Wall Street financier. He must have suffered like everybody else.

The reason he himself gave for his departure was more romantic. It seems, as usual, that there were a Mexican girl and a Bean mixed up together. In this case there was also a Mexican officer who meant to marry the girl. She being unwilling, Roy came to the rescue and carried her off himself. The officer dared him to the duelling ground. Accustomed as he was to duels, Roy killed his rival, but soon found he had started something he couldn't finish. The dead man's friends took the matter up, waylaid Roy, and hanged him to the nearest tree. The rope stretched, however, allowing his toes to touch the ground and giving him a chance to hold onto life until the girl he had rescued appeared and cut him down. After such a narrow squeak he decided he had better make tracks.

Whether it was woman trouble or bankruptcy or both that chased Roy out of California, one last fact should be mentioned. For the rest of his life he carried a red mark around his neck where the rope had burned his hide. Usually he covered it by tying a bandanna over it, but he showed it to his friends. As a result of the same episode his neck was always stiff as a board and he had to turn his whole body when he wished to turn his head. Usually he looked out of the corner of his eye at anything approaching from the side, not shifting himself unless he had to, a mannerism which made him seem like a much stealthier character than he really was.

WAR IN NEW MEXICO

IF ROY BEAN could come back to New Mexico today he would recognize Old Mesilla. In eighty years it has given up much of its life but none of its character. Forty miles from El Paso and two from Las Cruces it is a hundred years from them both in point of time. A handful of venerable brown adobes dreaming under the great alamo trees, the church in the middle, are all that remain of what was once a capital city, but History stands on every corner and peeps from every window.

When Roy's horse limped down the dusty main street in 1858 or '59 Mesilla was a lively place. It was the half-way station where the east-bound and west-bound stages met as they went jouncing across the continent. It was the trading center of a vast area just opening up for development. Its streets and saloons were crowded with teamsters, miners, Indians, gamblers, prospectors, settlers, fugitives from justice, and just plain people.

Roy liked Mesilla at once. It was the sort of place the Bean brothers always headed for—a frontier community on the make where pushing Americans could get theirs without too much regulation and interference.

Sam was easily located. His loud voice, audible for half a mile when the wind was right, would have given him away in the absence of other signs. Roy did not have to rely on his ears, however, for Sam was an important person in Mesilla and ran one of the biggest places in town. It was a combination store, eating house, saloon, hotel, and gambling den, and his business netted him, he said, two hundred dollars a day in flush times (it is admitted by all that he loved a good story). Besides his store, he operated a freighting and hauling business, carting people, building material, food supplies, furniture—anything—as far as his customers could desire and pay for.

And that was not all Sam had to be proud of. Like his brothers he dearly loved to shine in public office, and when Roy arrived Sam was draped in an official toga big enough for a dozen ordinary men. He was serving his second term as Sheriff of Dona Ana County. That doesn't sound extraordinary, but it was. This was just after the Gadsden Purchase and Dona Ana County stretched hundreds of miles to the west into what is now Arizona. And Sam was the boss of it all, or should have been.

It was really a job for a dozen men. Sam complained that he was almost powerless as an officer of the law because by the time he was able to reach the scene of a crime in the remote corners of his county, the criminals had crossed the border and spent two pleasant weeks in Mexico.

Sam was a pretty bright fellow, perhaps the best of the Bean brothers mentally, and he did the intelligent thing. He allowed the laws of Natural Selection and Survival of the Fittest to operate in his territory. He didn't even carry a gun.

For the third time in ten years Roy somersaulted from destitution into prosperity by means of a brother. Sam said later that Roy was "practically naked" when he arrived at Mesilla and didn't even have an extra shirt.

"But he was my brother," said Sam, "so I got him some clothes, had him shaved and cleaned up, and gave him some spending money."

Some responsibilities came Roy's way too. With his experience at the Headquarters he was able to make himself useful and the brothers began to be spoken of as partners. In 1861 they decided to expand the business and picked out Pinos Altos as a promising site.

Pinos Altos was a bonanza mining camp in the mountains above Silver City and a hundred-odd miles from Mesilla. It sprang up in 1861, boomed briefly, and then went into a decline for the period of the Civil War. Roy and Sam were there early and set up in business on Main Street. Copies of the Mesilla *Times* for 1861 carry their advertisement as dealers in "merchandise and liquors," adding the further lure of "a fine billiard table."

There was money in it for a few months. Then the Civil War broke out. The miners began leaving to enlist in one army or the other. The Indians crept closer and the boom petered out. In the fall of 1861 the Apaches made an especially fierce attack on Pinos Altos. Fifteen Apaches and three miners were killed, and only a few white men were willing to remain after that to risk their scalps for gold. Among the heroic souls who stayed Roy and Sam Bean were not numbered.

There was enough to keep them occupied back in Mesilla, what with one thing and another. They had five lawsuits on their hands that fall—attachments and replevins —and then there was more and more feeling about the war. It took some time for the county to get worked up to serious action, but hot words were spoken and blows were struck. Then there were riots and street fights. Eventually a Confederate flag flew in the main street, the Union men were invited to go elsewhere, and Mesilla was proclaimed Territorial Capital of what the organizers called Arizona.

Nothing could have pleased the Bean brothers better.

Sam told his friends long after the war that he had tried to be neutral in the interest of business, but of course nobody could be neutral and besides the Beans were from Kentucky.

Roy was actively partisan and did some unofficial military service for the South. Major Bell, who kept up a correspondence with him for forty years and is usually reliable, says that Roy "assisted in organizing a company of Confederate sympathizers that called themselves the Free Rovers. Others called them the Forty Thieves. After the failure of the Texas campaign in New Mexico, the Forty Thieves disbanded."

The Free Rovers had no muster roll, no formal organization, and no connection with the enlisted forces of the Confederacy. There is no record of their activities, and the natural deduction is that they were a very informal group welded together by love of country and of portable property belonging to somebody else.

A year before his death Roy loosened up a little and discussed this part of his life with a well-known collector of Texana, A. J. Sowell. He was "identified with the forces of the Confederacy under General Canby," reported Sowell in the San Antonio *Express*.

Roy Bean was attached to the command of General John R. Baylor as spy and scout and was present when General Baylor, through stratagem, captured 800 Federal troops in a deep canyon where they had been located by Bean, and demanded their surrender, stating that the balance of his men, 1000 in number with artillery, were in sight. These men, 250 in number, were scattered over several miles of country coming in squads and raising a great dust. The Federal officer surrendered, but after the arms were stacked and the fact of the small force of Baylor disclosed, his chagrin and anger knew no bounds. He cursed and raved and, as the saying is, tore his hair. Bean speaks in high terms of General Baylor and says that while he was rough and to some seemed to be over-bearing, his judgment was good, his bravery and confidence in himself to accomplish things were sublime. The artillery of General Baylor as mentioned above consisted of one swivel gun mounted on a mule which always knocked the mule down when it was fired.

In spite of the shrewdness and heroism of Bean and Baylor, New Mexico could not be held for the Confederacy. The little army from Texas won the battle of Glorietta and then retired southward, taking a backwash of Confederate sympathizers along. Included in this backwash were the Beans.

Roy seems to have left first, and there is a story about that. Sam Bean told it to his friend Joe Dwyer one time when Mr. Dwyer was resting from his labors as customs inspector on the International Bridge between El Paso and Juarez.

"I had to go to Santa Fe on business," said Sam, "so I showed Roy how to open the safe, told him to put the money in it every night, and give the gamblers their little sacks in the morning. Well, I got back a few days later and Roy wasn't there. The safe was locked and those gamblers were about ready to cut Roy's throat and mine too. I opened up the safe and it was plumb empty—not a penny inside—and maybe you think I didn't have to find some money quick to satisfy those gamblers!

"There was a good horse and saddle missing too. I never did see much of Roy after that."

Roy gave his own version of the flight from New

Mexico, omitting mention of locked safes and missing saddle horses, to A. J. Sowell:

"Judge Bean was in several Indian fights in New Mexico and finally started with a wagon train to Texas. Following the train was Mr. Van Riper with 300 head of mares, which he was trying to get to Texas. On the way the Indians attacked them, coming from the rear. Van Riper saw them coming and rushed his stock up to the wagons and the battle was fought with no loss to the whites except in animals, four of Van Riper's mares being killed. After the train moved on, the Indians had a feast on the dead bodies of the stock, building large fires and roasting them, meanwhile dancing and singing, all of which could be seen and heard from the train in camp at night. On the next day the Indians overtook the train again and had another fight and as before were beaten off, but killed some more of Van Riper's stock and had another feast. This was the last seen of them."

Roy went to earth in San Antonio which was thoroughly Southern and a beehive of Confederate business. The Yankees were blockading the coast and a great deal of exporting and importing was carried on through Old Mexico. The hauling business looked good to Roy. Soon he was running cotton down the river to the British ships ready off Matamoros, and bringing back supplies to the Confederate soldiers and civilians. For the rest of his twenty years in San Antonio he combined the occupation of teamster with several less laborious ways of making a living.

Sam Bean spent the war years in San Antonio too, but when the fighting was over he made up his mind to go back to New Mexico. Back he went and found that his glory had departed. His property had been libelled for treason;

Union men had bought life interests in the "Rebel estates," including his; he had nothing left.

One story survives showing how a Bean, even a Bean by marriage, could meet such a situation. When Mrs. Sam Bean found her house occupied by Union squatters, she put on a sad face, knocked on the door, and asked if she might come in and look at the old home where she had lived so long and in such happy days. Of course she might come in. And when once she got inside they never got her out till the place was hers again.

Still things were not the same for Mr. and Mrs. Sam Bean. After a while they moved to Silver City and then to Las Cruces, where Sam died nearly forty years later and where his memory is still green. He was a peace-loving man compared with Roy, but was pugnacious in argument and could be heard all up and down Main Street when he ran into tough opposition. He used to go to the Methodist church in his later years and functioned as a sort of ministerial alarm clock, yawning loud and long when the usual time limit for sermons was passed.

He wrote down many of his memories, some of which he published. Among his unpublished papers are versions of several of the Roy Bean yarns. One of them begins: "You may have graduated at Yale or Harvard and carry a number of diplomas, but if you have not seen or heard of Judge Roy Bean of Texas you are groping in darkness and there yet remains a large space to be filled in your classical head."

It appears that neither empty safes nor missing horses nor years of separation could destroy the bond between one Bean and another.

"THE DEFENDANT, ROY BEAN——"

SAN ANTONIO is today the closest thing to an old Spanish town in the United States. Seventy-five years ago it was as Mexican as chili peppers. Patriarchal clans with melodious names ran the commercial and social life of the place in the old-fashioned way. Politics was a family matter. There were a great many Germans and Frenchmen and Americans who moved in their own tight little circles, but everybody picked up the Spanish language and slid into Spanish ways.

Roy Bean liked that. He liked the way people loafed half a day at a time on the shady side of an adobe house telling stories. He liked the smoke and clatter of the *cantinas* in the evening. He liked the green, mesquite-studded Texas landscape on which the town sat so comfortably— the clear streams of water puttering cheerfully along the busiest streets—the *lavanderas* washing clothes on the banks —the small boys scandalizing the washwomen by swimming naked under their noses.

He liked the people—the proud men and the beautiful girls with their brilliant eyes and the soft, dark bloom on their cheeks.

He liked the Mexican view that every man had a right to his own vices.

And so he left the Frenchmen and the Germans and the Americans to enjoy their own society while he went Mexican. He naturally lost caste by it when the Mexican element gave up its predominance, and he is not spoken of with much respect by the few surviving Americans who knew him in those days, but for the first few years, at least, he got along all right. There wasn't so much race prejudice then, and besides the war kept people from worrying too much about minor matters.

Everything seemed to come his way at first. Next to running a saloon he liked best to work with horses and wagons, and freighters were just then in great demand. The railroad was still many years off and every day the monstrous, white-topped freight wagons rolled majestically off to Laredo or Brownsville or Brazos Santiago.

Perhaps the business wasn't quite what it had been when the caravans pulled out regularly for El Paso. There weren't any soldiers for escort duty now, and the Comanches lurked hungrily all along the western road, hoping that God would send them just one wagon train. Still business was pretty good, for the Yankee blockade off the Gulf coast made hauling from Mexico necessary and profitable.

All in all Roy found blockade running a very good way of making a living. For one thing every bale of cotton which got to England was a trick won from the North and Roy always enjoyed putting something over on the Damyankees. There was also the money. How it rolled in! In a remarkably (you might say suspiciously) short time he had accumulated several thousand dollars' worth of property in teams and wagons. He bought good clothes and smoked expensive cigars and strutted to his heart's content. He used to brag, in leaner times, that in those early and prosperous days he had been in the habit of lighting his cigar with a five dollar bill.

Anybody who knew him will be sure that he found a way to burn his bill and have it too.

Women and timid men were afraid of him. His body was thicker now and he had the burly bulk of a prize fighter. His beard was black and thick and his sharp eyes glittered through the underbrush of hair and whiskers. To these natural advantages he added a mastery of the great game of bluff and a hair-trigger temper which could make him really dangerous sometimes. On the whole he wasn't as bad as he acted. He was just an ambitious American without much conscience, trying to get ahead in the only way he understood. So he outdrank the dryest, outswore the toughest, and outguessed the smartest.

It took several years for his victims to get stirred up enough to fight back, but the time came when they had put up with enough. As a result Roy broke out, in the year 1866, in a rash of lawsuits. Three separate times in the fall term of court he was brought to the bar of justice and three separate times he beat the rap.

The first misunderstanding went back to the fall of 1863 when the Yankee blockade was at its height. At that time an Irish storekeeper, Pat Milmo, decided he would make some money running cotton. Pat was the brother of Dan Milmo, who had fabulous estates in Mexico and was married to the daughter of the governor of Coahuila. Between them the brothers carried much political and financial weight, and Pat probably never dreamed he could be taken in by a newcomer in the freighting business. Anyway he hired Roy Bean and his wagons to haul forty bales of cotton from Harrisburg, where the railroad stopped, to Eagle Pass on the Rio Grande.

Roy loaded up and moved out on schedule, but when he got to Eagle Pass, the Milmo agent there said he had never heard of Mr. Bean or Mr. Bean's cotton and didn't care if he never did.

There was nothing to do but wait until orders to receive the cotton came through from Milmo to the agent.

As the days went by, Roy's temperature rose. He began figuring how much he would have been making if he had been working instead of waiting. He realized that if he expected compensation for those lost hours he would have to take it, so he picked up as much of his employer's property as he could lay hands on and drove off with it as soon as the cotton was disposed of.

For two years Milmo tried to get his property back and had no luck whatever. In the fall of 1866 he brought suit, indicating that three hundred and fifty dollars would compensate him for his losses.

Roy was equal to the occasion. Instead of planning a defensive campaign he attacked the enemy in the rear with a counter suit for two thousand dollars. Milmo, he said, had kept him waiting "for the term of thirteen days, until the 10th of January, 1864, to wit all of which time this defendant was detained with his load of grain to wit eight wagons and one hundred and eighty mules and thirteen employees. This defendant avers that each wagon with its owner was worth the sum of twelve dollars per day, making the sum of one hundred and fifty-six dollars per day which sum total for the thirteen days amounts to two thousand and twenty-eight dollars."

It was a nasty blow to Pat Milmo, suing for a measly three hundred and fifty dollars, to find himself in danger of losing two thousand. As a last, feeble, face-saving gesture he attempted to attach three hundred and fifty dollars' worth of Roy's property, but he was a beaten man and he knew it. Neither suit was pressed any farther.

As soon as the smoke of this encounter had cleared away, the firing commenced again from a new quarter.

This time Roy had to answer for his cool theft of half a wagon train.

The trouble began in March, 1866, when he rolled into San Antonio with eight large wagons bound for El Paso or some other town to the west. The wagons were "the property of the defendant Roy Bean," but he owed money on them and probably had been owing it for some time, if he was running true to form.

"Now is our chance!" said creditor Julien T. Romain to creditor Rafael Quintana. So they sent the sheriff trotting over to the yard where the wagons were waiting, while Roy and his mules got ready for the long haul west.

When Roy got back to the wagon yard he found himself eight wagons short.

By now everybody in San Antonio knew Roy Bean and knew what to expect from him—some sort of trick was certain to be up his sleeve. Therefore the sheriff and the creditors were amazed when nothing happened. April came and went, and Roy seemed indifferent. May passed, and he did nothing. June and July came along, and he gave a good imitation of a man paralyzed by the heat.

In August the creditors got permission to sell the property. Four wagons were actually disposed of and Julien T. Romain got his money. "Well," thought the sheriff, "it's too late for Bean to do anything now."

But it wasn't too late. As court opened a few days later, Rafael Quintana came rushing in with the news that Roy had driven calmly up to the yard where the wagons were impounded, hitched up to the four that were left, and creaked off to his original destination, supposedly El Paso.

Roy Bean, said Mr. Quintana, had "surreptitiously gotten possession of four of the said wagons, as your petitioner is informed and believes, without the consent of the sheriff or of your petitioner or petitioner's counsel." He added that "the said Roy Bean is now justly indebted to your petitioner in the sum of three hundred and four dollars; that he is about to remove his property beyond the county of Bexar in which this suit has been commenced and that the plaintiff will probably lose his debt."

Mr. Quintana was a good prophet—he did lose his debt. The case was in court again in 1868 and 1870 and probably was profitable only to the lawyers.

The third lawsuit filed against Roy in 1866 brought to light his unusual way of solving the housing problem. This he did by moving into a vacant building and squatting there, while the owner did everything but call out the National Guard to get him out.

In the year of the trial a San Antonian named Lively was the possessor of a small property on the banks of San Pedro Creek, the pretty stream which still winds indolently through the outskirts of San Antonio. Another man, named Wells, thought he would like to have a house in that location, made Lively an offer, and closed the deal. What was his surprise, when he went to take possession, to find the place already occupied by a bearded Bean who swore the property was his. Argument and persuasion failing, Wells and Lively took the matter before Justice Nordhaus who gave a judgment against Roy for sixty-three dollars and costs.

It seemed to Roy this time that the proper strategy would be a delaying action, so he asked for and was granted a new trial. This was in July; the second hearing was set for August 4th.

Justice Nordhaus and the rightful owners, however, determined to give Roy a dose of his own medicine. When the fourth of August rolled around they held the trial all

by themselves and sent the sheriff with a writ of execution
to take over the disputed property.

But Roy was not beaten yet. He applied in the District
Court for an injunction and got it, Nordhaus and Lively
being summoned to explain themselves. The court, fearful
of deception in the midst of all this treachery, even prepared a set of interrogatories for prospective witnesses,
hinting that somebody had faked a deed and demanding
plaintively to be told "If you know any fact or facts tending to show that the said property is the property of Roy
Bean."

The settlement finally reached was chuckled over in
San Antonio for years and was recalled by an *Express* reporter at the time of Roy's death forty years later:

"While residing here, Bean is said to have figured in a
famous lawsuit. Action was brought to eject him from certain property on the west side of town. As the legislation
proved somewhat vexatious, he finally agreed to com-
promise the suit, proposing that if the plaintiff would bear
all the expenses of moving his belongings to property in
the present site of Beanville and throw in a jug of his
favorite whiskey he would quit all claim to the subject
of suit. The proposition was accepted and San Antonio
was given a Beanville."

To this should be added the fact that Roy not merely
got what he wanted from Wells and Lively in exchange
for his removal; he also sold Mr. Wells forty mules and
horses, six wagons and harness, and one two-horse buggy
and harness. He got three thousand dollars in cash out of
the deal and never saw that much money again as long as
he lived.

BEAN OF BEANVILLE

FOR SIXTEEN YEARS after Wells and Lively moved him out, Roy Bean lived down on South Flores Street in his own private stronghold which soon came to be known as Beanville.

Anybody but Roy would have sacrificed a good deal to keep his name off the place. It was a poverty-stricken neighborhood, half cow pasture and half Mexican slum with scattered shacks here and there, the race track and fair grounds on one edge and Mr. Conner's general store in the middle. Some people called it Dogtown from the droves of curs maintained in a state of starvation by the natives. It was a sorry place in which to be the leading citizen, but that was Roy's way. He wanted the spotlight and he instinctively sought a level where he could have it all to himself with no rival to challenge him. He always preferred to strut in a yard just big enough for himself.

Inside of two months these tactics got him a wife. On October 28, 1866, he married Virginia Chavez, the eighteen-year-old daughter of Leandro M. Chavez, whose ranch was about a mile from San Antonio proper and close to Beanville. The Chavez were good substantial people. They didn't have much money, but they had an ancestry which went back, through the Chavez line, to an ancient noble family of Portugal and through another strain to one of the original thirteen families of aristocratic Canary Islanders who came to San Antonio in 1733 and

have never ceased to congratulate the town about it since.
It is hard to understand, in view of all this family pride,
why eighteen-year-old María Anastacia Virginia wanted
a forty-year-old rascal like Roy Bean. Perhaps she was
overcome by the reek of prosperity which he gave off.
A man who could sell out for three thousand dollars and
have three lawsuits in two months—he probably was,
had been, or might be a millionaire. Then too he talked
so long and loud of his glorious deeds that a wiser woman
than Virginia might well have imagined that a great man
was really within her grasp.

Of course she may even have liked him. He had plenty
of personal attractions when he was sober and cleaned up,
and he no doubt exerted himself to make a good impression.

Whatever her reason for the rash act, she soon found
out that being married to Roy was just a short cut to
trouble. Mr. and Mrs. Bean commenced a wandering and
precarious existence which was spent mostly in moving
from house to house, having babies, and trying to eat
regularly.

It would seem that Mrs. Bean woke up early to the
hard facts of her situation. Eight months after the wedding she had her husband in court. On July 12, 1867, she
and her mother affixed their marks (they couldn't, or
didn't, write) to a complaint stating that on June 19
Roy Bean "the life of a human being to wit the life of
Virginia Chavez de Bean did seriously threaten to take
contrary to the form of the statute in such case made and
provided and against the Peace and Dignity of the State."

Roy's lawyers did some very fine legal trapeze work
trying to have the case thrown out on various technical-
ities, but they failed. Then, knowing that feeling was
high against their client, they succeeded in getting a

change of venue to Boerne, thirty miles away and supposedly in neutral territory.

On December 10, 1868, the Law could find no further
reason for delay, and the case was dismissed. No transcripts
of evidence were kept.

Scandal, however, does not die easily, and Roy's assault case is now a part of the unwritten history of the
Texas bar. Story-telling lawyers still relate how Roy came
home one night in a very bad humor with his wife, whom
he found in bed. He finally became so angry that he
snatched a burning stick from the fireplace, pulled the
covers off the bed, and applied the blazing end of the
piece of wood to his wife's anatomy. She screamed to
heaven and ran home to her mother.

When she was able to move again without discomfort,
she filed suit for aggravated assault.

Roy's lawyer closed his defense by requesting the
plaintiff to show the jury the scars which she alleged she
had received. The request took her by surprise. She hesi-
tated; finally she refused. The judge lost patience and the
case was dismissed.

"You damn fool!" Roy snorted at his lawyer. "What
did you take a chance like that for? If the jury had seen
those scars, they'd have put me in jail for life and thrown
away the key."

"I didn't take much of a chance," returned the lawyer.
"You ought to know that a Mexican woman wouldn't
let a stranger look at her ankles if she could help it.
I knew she wouldn't lift her dress before that bunch of
men."

It may be that this story is pure folklore, for Mr. and
Mrs. Bean were soon living together again. There is probably some truth in it, for neither of them seemed to take

much satisfaction in the married state after that. Perhaps the birth of their first child had something to do with patching up the shattered family ties. They were back at the old Chavez homestead with her father when "Little Roy" came along. After that they kept a feeble home fire burning in various other houses here and there about San Antonio, but no matter where they lived they brought their discontents along with the other pieces of household furniture. Besides, the wolf was always snuffing at the crack under the door.

Nobody knows what happened to those three thousand dollars Roy had at the time of his marriage. Somehow they disappeared, and others didn't come easy. He tried one venture after another and succeeded only in getting deeper into poverty. The one thing he never ran out of was ideas.

At first he seems to have done some business in wood. Much of Beanville belonged to Wicks and Hickman, proprietors of a big freight line on which Roy found occasional employment. Wicks and Hickman encouraged him to keep an eye out for unauthorized digging of roots or chopping of trunks for firewood. This he regarded as a grant of monopoly for himself, and therefore felt free to engage to supply the firm of George Holmgreen and Sons, iron workers, with enough wood to stoke their furnaces. He was chased off two or three promising wood lots which happened to belong to owners jealous of their rights, and at last he solved the problem of supply by cracking down on the Mexican charcoal burners who operated out on Alazan and Leon creeks southwest of town where there were live oaks. These Mexicans leased tracts of land according to regulations, but often got away with a little poaching on adjoining acres. Roy found out about

this and developed a burning desire to see justice done.
He would visit the charcoal burners periodically (not too
often), accuse them of stealing, confiscate their wood, and
deliver it to the iron works. He took such a high tone
and talked so convincingly that his victims never dared
protest. In fact they habitually paid him twenty-five cents
a load for the privilege of cutting wood on somebody
else's land.

When the wood racket played out, Roy decided to go
into the dairy business. He overcame the initial difficulty
of providing cows by striking a bargain with a farmer
in Atascosa County who wished to sell his herd. Roy had
bought a shack and a couple of lots in 1872 for a hundred
and thirty dollars. The farmer wanted this property, so
they agreed to trade—the real estate for the farmer's thirty
cows. Roy, however, was never one to buy a pig (or a
cow) in a poke; he thought it was only right to ask for a
period of trial. The farmer could see that if the cows
didn't produce, he couldn't run a dairy.

The farmer saw, and Roy took the cows.

Feed was scarce that year and he had to be very eco-
nomical. Soon the cows showed signs of being under-
nourished. Then milk production fell off; profits went
down; and of course the less money he made, the less
feed Roy could pay for. The cows grew weak. Their
hungry bellowings became feebler. They began to die.

When the owner came around to take possession of
his real estate, presuming that the cows were doing all
right, he was told that the deal was off. "I only took them
on trial," said Roy, "and they proved to be worthless as
milkers."

A well-known Roy Bean anecdote from this period
concerns the dairy. Roy used to tell this one himself.

"When business was good," he would say, "and there wasn't enough milk to go around to all the customers, I used to dilute it a little. One day a well-known San Antonio judge knocked on the door. He said, 'If it's all the same to you I'd like to have my milk and water in separate vessels after this. I'll pay for both but I just would like to have them separate.'

" 'Why, what the hell's the matter, Judge?' I asked. 'What's wrong?'

" 'Well' he said, 'we found a minnow in the milk yesterday.'

" 'By God!' I said, 'that's what comes of watering them cows at the river.'

"But I had to break down and admit that I kept a bucket and dipper down by the bridge and sometimes I stopped and replenished my supply."

As a side line to his dairy, or perhaps as a successor to it, Bean did a little business in meat. When he needed some ready cash he would slip off to the outskirts of the city, butcher somebody's cow, and either peddle the meat from door to door or sell it in the little catch-all, hole-in-the-wall store which he operated. He even had a standing offer of five dollars to any boy who would bring him a stray horse or cow. All he asked was that the animal should be unbranded, and even then sometimes an angry owner would raid the corral and carry off his property over Roy's violent objections. Mostly the horses were sold and the cows were butchered. Roy would say in defense of the butchering, "No use for poor people to go hungry as long as rich people have fat cows." He was very fond of posing as a friend of "poor folks."

Once he took a chance and killed a yearling on land belonging to a rich resident of San Antonio. This man happened to be in the neighborhood, and seeing these strange goings on in his pasture he ambled over to take a look. There were Roy and his helper cooking part of the kill over a campfire. The hide was staked out near by, the hair up and the brand as plain as day. Roy said, "Howdy! Come and have a bite with us."

The man did so and took occasion to inform Roy of the facts about whose land he was on. He did not mention the branded hide. "I was pretty sure," he confessed afterwards, "that old Roy had some trick up his sleeve and I was afraid to call his hand."

When the man was gone, Roy spoke severely to his helper who had staked the hide out without turning the branded side down.

"Don't you know any better," he rasped, "than to stake that skin out with the hair side up? Always turn the brand down. Otherwise you'll ruin the hide."

The boy apologized and the incident was closed.

A similar situation occurred when two other land-owners rode up and found Roy in the act of skinning a beef on their acres.

"What's the brand on that hide?" demanded one of them.

"Get down and look at it," invited Roy.

This was the same thing in the West as asking a man to get down and be shot, as the men knew very well. They decided not to argue the point and rode away. Probably Roy was bluffing but they couldn't be sure. That was why Roy made his bluff stick so often—nobody was ever quite sure that it was really a bluff.

With his butchering, dairying, and woodcutting, Roy mixed in a little incidental saloon-keeping, though he never did sell much liquor in San Antonio. He opened up in the late 70's with a Frenchman named Grandjean. Their place was near San Antonio on the south bank of the Medina River. The venture did not pay, so Roy sold out to his partner and opened a bar at his house in Beanville. Here, too, he met with small success.

Meanwhile he was always glad to fall back on his second profession, which was driving horses. He worked sometimes for the big companies and he did small jobs for himself. For a while he made trips to Chihuahua by way of Presidio or El Paso, arduous and dangerous trips full of the perils of thirst and Indians, lasting for weary weeks and putting a man under severe mental strain while choking him with alkali dust.

Once he barely missed having his scalp lifted by Indians. This happened near Howard's Well, a station on the old Chihuahua Trail where there was good water and a small garrison of soldiers. It is now completely off the beaten track, but up until a few years ago anybody who was curious enough could go there and find scattered pieces of iron and charred wood in Howard's Draw, a few miles from the well, where the Comanches raided a wagon train in the early days.

On the evening of the massacre Roy Bean had brought his wagons and mules to a camping ground ten miles or so from Fort Howard. The wagons were properly placed; the mules were picking up a little supper; the sky was clear. Roy thought it would be safe for the *capitano* (himself) to pay a visit, so he jogged off to the fort. As he rode in he noticed a Mexican freighting outfit camped not far off. The soldiers were glad to see him. Corks popped and bottles gurgled. The jollification had been going on for some time when a soldier on watch came in and reported a fire in Howard's Draw a couple of miles off. Everybody looked. The blaze was sharp against the early morning sky, and cries and shots floated faintly to their ears. The Mexican caravan was being wiped out.

"Injuns," said Roy, and he rode off before the soldiers had fully realized what was going on.

It was after daylight when Roy got back to his wagons and found everything safe. By the time breakfast was over the sun was up. At that moment two hunted human beings staggered into camp—a man and a woman. They were the only survivors of the massacre. Everybody else was dead.

Roy was curious about how they escaped, but they were very reluctant to give any details. Finally it came out that the woman was the discontented wife of one of the teamsters and she had arranged a meeting at daylight with the mule wrangler. They had risen while everyone else still slept, slipped out of camp, slid over the edge of the bank down into the draw, and lain down in the grass. That saved their lives, for just then the Indians struck. While the shooting and yelling were going on over their heads, they stole away and got off.

Bean saw how matters stood. He chased the Mexican man out of camp and told the woman to get into his wagon.

When Roy was an old man he sometimes used to recall this episode. "I sure ran that Mexican off," he would chuckle. Then he would add: "But I don't do that way any more. I've quit all that now."

In August Santleben's book, *A Texas Pioneer*, there is a record showing that Anastacio Gonzales and eight Mexican teamsters were killed at Howard's Well in 1872. The lady in Roy's wagon was probably the wife of one of them.

At last the long-distance freighting business ceased to pay, like all Roy's other ventures. He said once that he stopped hauling into Chihuahua "because my horse wouldn't drink water in Mexico." That would mean he had some trouble and wouldn't risk going back. Everett Lloyd says it was because of a fight. Roy killed a Mexican in a back-alley brawl of some kind and had to be smuggled out of town under a load of hides. Whatever was behind it, the hauling business gradually petered out for him. Even his equipment went to pieces steadily until he had only the weakest excuse for a wagon train left.

Vinton James of Uvalde, who hired him to come out and haul some wool in 1880, describes his equipment as "the sorriest I ever beheld."

"The six wagons were rickety. The team to draw same were an equal number of jackasses and emaciated horses. The harness consisted of ropes, leather and rawhide thongs, chains and ill-fitted collars for the jackasses. In case of rain there was not a wagon sheet. As the weather was rainy I refused to allow him to leave. He had turned his teams into my horse pasture where the grass was fine. He stayed with me almost a week to recuperate. It surely was a comical sight to see his little jacks hitched up with horses, with my wool aboard on the way to San Antonio."

That was how Roy had come down in twenty years— from the gay caballero in red-topped boots to the "comical sight" on the streets of San Antonio! It was the most humiliating thing that could possibly have happened to an egoist like Roy Bean. But there was no way out that he could think of. He had to swallow his pride before he and his family could swallow anything else.

A group of deputy United States marshals camped on some disputed property near Roy's place in 1875 and he

lost no time in starting a borrowing acquaintance. The
late Joe Dwyer of El Paso was one of them and used to
tell how Roy would mosey over to the camp for the permanent loan of a cup of sugar or coffee, or anything else
he could pick up. They found him likable, however,
and sometimes they gathered for a dance in his one-room,
dirt-floored house. The boys from the camp would bring
in the raw materials and Mrs. Bean would cook up a
supper. The Mexican girls in the neighborhood were delighted to be asked as partners. Sometimes it was two
o'clock in the morning before anybody went home.

Such pleasures broke the monotony, but they couldn't
give Roy anything like content. His troubles continued to
increase as his dollars diminished. He felt more and more
resentful of his wife, and she no doubt returned the feeling with interest. Often he thought of escape. There must
be some place in the world where there weren't any shrill-
voiced, complaining women, and where there wasn't a
policeman on every street corner pining to arrest somebody.

That reminded him of what people were saying about
the wild country in West Texas—"No law west of the
Pecos." Maybe out there it would be like the old days
in California. "I'd like to move out to that country," he
said to himself. "No law west of the Pecos, eh? Well, God
knows there's too much law around Santone."

END OF A CHAPTER

THERE ARE TIMES in everybody's life when it would be a pleasure to take off for Siberia or Timbuctoo if only there weren't so many things in the way, and so it was with Roy Bean. There was every reason why he should be somewhere else and every reason why he couldn't. He was too old just to pick up and go—too poor to make a new start without help. It took him four more years to break loose.

He would have sought refuge in drink, but it takes money to stay drunk for any length of time and money was scarce. About the only place he could be sure of steady liquor was Conner's grocery store, and there he made his headquarters. And that brings Mr. and Mrs. Conner into the picture.

T. E. Conner was an energetic Irishman who had set up in business in Beanville seven years before and had become the Big Man of the community. Teamsters trading to the south made his wagon yard their headquarters. Everybody in Beanville bought groceries over his counter. His neighbors elected him alderman and the rest of San Antonio knew him as the Mayor of Beanville.

A man in his position has to play for the good will of the public, and Mr. Conner knew a trick or two which helped him to stay popular. In his back room he kept a demijohn of whiskey, and whenever a mule driver about to leave on a long trip stopped at the yard for supplies,

Mr. Conner would outfit him and, as a token of regard, would throw in a flask of whiskey for his saddle bags. Roy knew all the teamsters and belonged to the fraternity himself. No whiskey bottle ever left the wagon yard without moistening the whiskers of Roy Bean.

Conner didn't mind this very much but Mrs. Conner did. She was a Northern woman, a little uncomfortable in her Texas environment, and Roy Bean scared her. His whiskers and dirt, his gleaming eyes and gruff voice, his love of whiskey and his rough talk—well, she wished he would hang around somebody else's wagon yard.

Occasionally she heard him grumbling about hard times and the way things used to be, and one day Mrs. Conner got her courage up and asked him why he didn't move.

"Takes money," said Roy.

"You could sell out."

"Who'd want to buy what I've got?"

"I would."

Roy looked interested. "Any strings to it?" he asked.

"Well, I won't buy your property unless you leave the country. That's what you want to do, isn't it?"

And so, unexpectedly, Roy had his chance to move on, but now he wasn't sure he wanted to go. His reason was characteristic of him and a few days later, in a conversation with Mrs. Conner, he let her see what it was. "This is my town," he said. "It's named after me, and as soon as I've gone it'll be Connersville or something. I don't like that."

Lazy and low as he had become, Roy was still related to the young Kentuckian in red-topped boots who had run the show at the Headquarters Saloon thirty years before. He was willing to sacrifice almost anything to stay in the center of the stage no matter how small and mean the stage was. He had to be Somebody. As long as he lived he would be looking for a short cut to distinction, and at the moment his name attached to Beanville was about the only distinction he had left.

Mrs. Conner saw this and found a way to solve the problem.

"If you'll sell and go away," she said, "I'll see that Beanville stays Beanville. I'll even put Beanville at the head of my letters when I write to somebody."

That was more like it, and Roy went off to think it over some more.

What could he do? Go back to driving mule teams? No. The time for that was about over. Already the railroad had reached San Antonio and was pushing westward. In 1877 he himself had attended the celebration which took place on the arrival of the first train at the San Antonio station. Well oiled with whiskey from Conner's grocery, he had danced a joyful jig on a flat car and ever since had felt a yearning interest in the construction of the line.

Almost every day the papers reported rapid progress: July 14, 1881—"Building fast west of Medina." July 20 —"The railroad crosses the Frio." Aug. 4—"The railroad is four miles past Hondo."

There was something going on out there that he understood—grading camps, teamsters, hard work (for somebody else), hard men, hard women. The frontier back again. A hair-trigger life where "them that shot quickest lived longest" and where foxy lawyers and nosy police officers could not upset the schemes of a smart Kentuckian.

Just how to hitch his wagon to the railroad was not clear to Roy, however, until his friend W. N. Monroe, one of the biggest grading contractors for the "Sunset" (soon to become a part of the Southern Pacific system), asked him why he didn't start a saloon at one of the construction camps.

"That's a good idea," said Roy. "Maybe I will."

"I'll help out on the equipment," offered Monroe.

The next step was to make a bargain with Mrs. Conner, which was soon done. She got everything Roy owned for nine hundred dollars, and he got his freedom. With this stake and the help of contractor Monroe, Roy provided himself with a tent, a barrel of whiskey, some bottled beer, and a little incidental equipment. He put his children in charge of Mr. and Mrs. Simon Fest, Jr., friends of his. In a short time he had his gear loaded on a wagon. Then all he had to do was head west down the right of way toward the "end of track" which was crawling relentlessly toward the Pecos River.

And thus it was that Roy Bean started on his last adventure when most men would have been glad to relax on the sunny side of the house. He was fifty-six years old but his greatest moments were still ahead and he felt ready for them. His thatch of hair, thick as sheep's wool, was only just beginning to show threads of gray. His craft and cunning were as acute as formerly. Perhaps he looked with a little less interest at the shapely Mexican girls who bought their *abarrotes* at Conner's grocery—but he still looked. It was not too late to start life over.

There were a dozen camps along the line of the railroad and Roy may have stopped at one or all of them. It was a simple matter to pack up the tent and the bottles when a crew moved on to a new location. The railroad itself was moving fast, however, and by the spring of 1882 he was across the Pecos River in a wilderness which partly justified General Sheridan's statement that if he owned Hell and Texas he would rent Texas and live in Hell.

WITH NOTHING MUCH LEFT TO LIVE
FOR ROY BEAN HEADS WEST AGAIN AND
BECOMES THE LAW WEST OF THE PECOS.

And so I went and settled myself down on the head of Shoal Creek. We remained here some two or three years without any law at all; and so many bad characters began to flock in upon us, that we found it necessary to set up a sort of temporary government of our own.

My judgments were never appealed from, and if they had been they would have stuck like wax as I gave my decisions on the principles of common justice and honesty between man and man, and relied on natural born sense, and not on law learning to guide me; for I had never read a page of a law book in my life.

THE AUTOBIOGRAPHY OF DAVY CROCKETT.

THE PECOS COUNTRY

THE PECOS COUNTRY was and is a savage region. Even to-day its endless miles of nothing weigh down the soul of the traveler as he hurries through it at seventy-five miles an hour. Imagine how it seemed to men who had to cross it on horseback or behind a team of mules sixty years ago!

Rolling hills of rock rubble and thin soil, lonely and naked as they were the day after the Creation. Monstrous canyons gouged out by the Pecos and the Rio Grande hundreds of feet straight down through the primeval rock. Smaller canyons and arroyos crisscrossing the rugged slopes, their bleached and rocky beds dry as bones most of the year but raging like Niagara after a rain. Over all a mournful wind continually blowing—moving gently on the level places; racing and shrieking down the canyons like an army charging out of hell. That was and is the Pecos country.

Life goes on under difficulties. Ghostly gray coyotes, weird little lizards, shy desert birds flit aside and disappear like timid visitors from another world. Rattlesnakes gorge and coil and send out the warning of death. Bears and mountain lions hole up in rocky dens and live by tooth and claw.

Every living thing seems prepared to fight for its life. Even the plants go armed; and hardly a shrub can be found without a spine or fang of some sort. The heavy spikes of the Spanish dagger are sharp and stiff enough to impale a man. The prickly pear is needled like the porcupine. The most innocent and harmless-looking bushes are likely to have wicked stilettos lurking among their tender green leaves. Even their names have edge and point—cat claw and ocotillo and crown of thorns.

And yet some people love this barren wilderness. Its very bigness and barrenness give them a sense of freedom —a firmer grip on reality. And besides, the desert has its tender moments for anyone who is not too much in a hurry to wait for them. All the year there are sunsets and sunrises which sweep the sky for a few minutes with royal robes. In the spring millions of delicate plants grow green and blossom, throwing rich carpets of color over the bony ridges of the land. When the tough rind of the earth begins to warm to the approaching summer the dagger plant hangs out a great lantern of waxy white blossoms. The yucca sends up a tall spike which bursts into a foam of white bells wonderful to behold. The prickly pear sprouts fabulous yellow petals on its thorny pads. The most wretched little pincushion of a cactus crouching among the rocks will suddenly hold up a scarlet bloom so savagely beautiful that it takes the breath away.

Even the hills of stone rolling in huge swells like a petrified ocean have a charm of their own. Blasted and ruinous as they seem close at hand, they soften with distance. Their rugged contours grow gentle, and their thin garment of creosote bushes, cactus, and weedy plants looks on far slopes like a sprinkling of soft, greenish mold.

Always there is a spacious, honest quality about it all— a hard country, maybe, but not like some places where cruelty and starvation lurk among the orange blossoms.

In 1882 this Pecos country looked just as it does now. The wagon roads which threaded a dusty way across it were lost in the immensity, just as the railroads and automobile highways are today. The sheep and cattle ranches are more plentiful now, but they seem just as solitary and alone in the waste of rock and sky as they did before the railroad came. The breed of men which grows there is still hardy and tough—perhaps as hardy and tough as the wild crew that rode in on the back of the iron stallion in 1882, scaring the lizards and coyotes with strange oaths and the clang of pickaxes.

Yes, the Pecos country still looks the same, but people no longer say, as they did then, "West of the Pecos there is no law and west of El Paso there is no God."

VINEGAROON

THE HARDY HOODLUMS who built the railroad concentrated in great numbers along the Pecos in the spring
of 1882. They camped beside the right of way in one of
the worst tent-town Babylons the West ever knew. It consisted of several different shack-and-tent communities.
Farthest west, some twenty miles from the Pecos and
hovering on the banks of the Rio Grande, was Eagle's
Nest, so called because of a collection of rubbish visible
on the wall of the Rio Grande Canyon which was used
for domestic purposes by one of the local eagles. Nothing
is left of Eagle's Nest now, but a permanent settlement
sprang up around a water tank several hundred yards up
the river when the railroad was completed in 1883. This
place was officially christened Langtry by Roy Bean, who
set up his frame castle there and ruled the surrounding
country for many years.

A few miles east of Eagle's Nest was Soto City which
sprang up and then sprang down again in the summer of
1882. Still farther east, in the angle made by the Pecos and
the Rio Grande, was the largest and wickedest community
of all—the tent town of Vinegaroon. This place was named
after a repulsive but non-poisonous insect found all
over the West. It should be said at once that the town was
like the insect in being repulsive, but nobody could say
that it was non-poisonous.

Vinegaroon consisted of an irregular and scattered collection of tents strung along the west bank of the Pecos, with subdivisions reaching for a mile or so down toward the Rio Grande. There was a good deal of blasting, drilling, tunnelling, and grading necessary for the part of the road bed (now abandoned) which dropped into the Rio Grande Canyon for a few precarious miles; consequently a large force was maintained at Vinegaroon for some time.

Being composed almost entirely of flimsy canvas structures, the town disappeared from the face of the earth once the construction work was over. A few old bottles, a broken tool, a Chinese coin, sometimes remind the passer-by of what was, but the only real relic of Vinegaroon is a ruined stone enclosure near the hamlet of Shumla just a short way from the place where the automobile road comes up out of the Pecos Canyon. There is a good deal of speculation about what it was used for, but everybody in those parts knows that it was built by Roy Bean. Roy told a friend one time why he laid those rocks together. "I had so much trouble," he said, "with thieves breaking into my place I finally threw up four stone walls and pitched my tent over them. After that I had some peace."

The stone corral does not mark Roy's first stopping place after he crossed the Pecos. His first camp was on the west bank of the river right beside the ford. At this time there was no bridge and everybody had to use the Bullis crossing just above the junction of the Pecos and the Rio Grande. The concentration of travelers at this point looked promising, so Roy set himself up as a one-man information bureau, guide, supply officer, and friend to all who passed that way. He figured that his wisdom and guidance were worth money to any traveler, and maybe he was right.

Supposing a man didn't want any of Roy's wisdom and

guidance? Well, there were lots of thieves and rustlers in the country and like as not the traveler would awaken the next morning and find his stock missing.

Then Roy would appear.

"You lost your mules? Too bad! Well, I warned you. Maybe it ain't too late to get them back yet. How much would you pay if I was to find those mules for you?"

If the payment could be arranged satisfactorily, the mules came back.

This, of course, provided small pickings, and before long Roy moved on. For several months he hovered between Eagle's Nest and Vinegaroon. Eagle's Nest seems to have attracted him first, and he published a notice of his new location in the San Antonio *Express* for July 27, 1882:

A Card from Roy Bean, from Beanville
  On the Banks of the Rio Grande,
  Eagle's Nest Springs, Pecos Co.,
  H'd Quarters Depot Saloon,
  Munroe's Camp No. 6,
  July 25, 1882

I would announce to my friends and the public in general, that I have opened another saloon at the above place, where can be found the best of wines, liquors and cigars that the house of A. B. Frank and Co. affords. My saloon is at the meeting point of the great Southern Pacific and Western extension of the Sunset railway. No other saloon within a mile and a half from my place, and visitors will always find a quiet, orderly place, where they can get a good drink. My saloon is inside the camp. In connection with my saloon I have a good restaurant, where one can at all times get a good "square meal." This place has been selected and land purchased for a grand depot, and will be built so soon as the two roads are graded to this point. The selection was made by

W. N. Munroe, the king of R.R. contractors. The water is good and the scenery grand. Will be pleased to see any of my friends at all times.

Roy Bean
Beanville

Dreams of prosperity to follow the establishment of the "grand depot," it seems, was the lure which brought Roy to Eagle's Nest. There was also another attraction. On the last day of June, 1882, Captain Oglesby of the Texas Rangers set up a "permanent camp" there, leaving Corporal Shannonhouse in charge of the men who brought in offensive desperadoes. Roy Bean was the man the desperadoes were brought to, and the reports of the ranger detachment show that his justice court was functioning soon after the permanent camp was set up.

It is usually supposed that his judgeship was his own idea and the romancers who have built up the Bean saga to its present mythical proportions like to leave it at that. They like to paint old Roy as a "self-appointed" J.P., who set himself up in the law business and made it stick. They love to picture him as playing a lone hand in a tough country and surviving by sheer guts. A well-known writer, describing Bean's career in the *Saturday Evening Post* in 1931, assured his readers solemnly that "as a matter of cold legal fact Roy Bean was no more justice of the peace than the first jack rabbit to be met in the Big Bend brush."

Well, it wasn't quite as romantic as that, but the plain truth about what happened is almost as exciting as the more familiar fiction.

We begin with Eagle's Nest, Soto City, and Vinegaroon. Those tent cities west of the Pecos were God-awful places. The migratory towns which kept even with the End of Track were known in the West as "Hell on Wheels" and that was, if anything, an understatement. They were soaked in blood, whiskey, and corruption. Mostly male, they nevertheless nourished a few women who squalled and fought and hustled in the dives and dance halls of the camps. Some were well known all over the West—for instance, Rowdy Kate Lowe, late of Tombstone, who was brought into Roy Bean's justice court on August 21, 1882, by the rangers.

The men were mostly workers. In the summer of 1882 there were 8000 of them concentrated within a space of some twenty miles. Many were foreigners who scarcely spoke English. The rest included youths from New England who wanted to make a stake in the West, runaway farm boys from the prairie states, and all the other odds and ends of humanity who show up in such places. There were even a few Chinamen, though most of the Orientals used on this railroad were employed by the Southern Pacific and were working east from El Paso toward their own End of Track. Whatever their origin, the workers on a railroad grading project are traditionally good pickings for sharpers, and naturally these attracted a choice collection of poker men, wheel men, monte men, dice men, faro men, and men who robbed without the formality of gambling equipment. They all buzzed in like a swarm of bluebottle flies, and trouble moved in with them.

The junction of the Gulf, Harrisburg & San Antonio (or Sunset) and the Southern Pacific was scheduled to take place somewhere between Eagle's Nest and Vinegaroon, and as the two lines drew closer, the tension in the camps rose. Work and vice speeded up together. As more jobs were finished and more men laid off, the devil found more work for idle hands to do. Greater numbers of corpses per day were buried in the rocky ground. The dance halls grew noisier and the human leeches grew plumper.

The railroad contractors reflected that all this was happening in the United States of America among civilized people in the year 1882. They decided to ask for help, and the result was a letter from Major Converse to the Adjutant General of Texas (chief of the Texas Rangers) dated June 6, 1882. "Our contractors on the Pecos are daily annoyed by a lot of hard cases, and the only way we can maintain order will be to have 8 or 10 of your men at the Pecos," said Major Converse. "Please aid us if you can do so."

General King could do so. He ordered Lieutenant L. P. Sieker of Co. D, in camp near Uvalde, to send a detachment to handle the emergency and instructed Captain Oglesby, in camp at Cotulla seventy-five miles farther to the southeast, to move over and take permanent charge. The rangers moved in according to instructions and by the end of June were beginning to get the situation in hand, but it was hard going. They had to clean out places like Soto City which had nine saloons and only one store. "Acts of violence," they reported, "are of daily occurrence." There was only one deputy sheriff in the whole God-forsaken country and no justice of the peace.

Captain Oglesby wrote General King a letter about it:

Eagle's Nest, Pecos Co. Tex.
July 5th 1882

Gen. W. H. King
Austin Texas
   Sir:
   Upon my arrival here on the 29th I proceeded to visit all the railroad Camps and scout the country thoroughly. I fond

six of Lieut. Seker's men here under Sergt. Tom Carson and
feel in duty bound to say the Sergt and men have done
excellent work, puting things to wright and keeping the
roughfs strait.

There is the worst lot of roughfs, gamblers, robbers, and
pickpockets, collected here I ever saw, and withou the
immediate presents of State troops this class would prove a
great detriment towards the completion of the road. There
is nothing here for Rangers to do but hold this rough element
in subjection and controll them. The majority of the railroad
Camps are in Pecos county. This immediate section being
two hundred miles from Stockton the nearest jurisdiction
Court of Justice and the consequent minor offences go un-
punished but I hope to remedy that in a few days by having
a Magistrate appointed for this Precincts.

An extra reason for Captain Oglesby's desire for a justice of the peace appears in the following entry in his
monthly report to the Adjutant General:

Aug. 5th. Pvt Lindsey returned from Ft. Stockton via Ft.
Davis. Assisted sheriff in conveying prisoners from Eagle's
Nest to Ft. Stockton. Out 12 days. Marched 600 miles.

Six hundred miles and twelve days' time! No wonder
Oglesby wanted a justice of the peace appointed. And he
might have found a worse candidate than Roy Bean.

The records of Pecos County show that Roy Bean was
appointed Justice of the Peace on August 2, 1882, by the
Commissioners' Court and that he qualified by submitting
a thousand-dollar bond on December 6, 1882.

Long before that bond was filed, however, the Law
West of the Pecos was in active operation. On July 25, a
week before he was legally appointed, the rangers brought
Joe Bell, charged with aggravated assault, into his court-

room at Eagle's Nest. And that, incidentally, is the only real basis for describing him as a "self-appointed" justice of the peace.

In September the detachment of rangers was moved to Vinegaroon and Roy went along to be where he was worse needed.

Vinegaroon was so notoriously tough at this time that an ordinary citizen took his life in his hands to visit the place, particularly if he had any valuables along.

John J. Stevens of San Antonio was secretary and treasurer for the G.H. & S.A., and it became his duty in 1882 to take a payroll to Vinegaroon to pay off some men who were threatening to strike. Carefully keeping his secret and never relaxing his death-grip on the little black bag containing $300,000 in fifty-dollar bills, he and his ranger escort—one ranger—set out. The special train consisting of coach and engine arrived at the end of the track about one A.M., and he found at once that it was in the shank of the evening for Vinegaroon. It was Saturday night and dawn was far away.

As he left his train, in a very doubtful frame of mind, he was greeted by a volley of shots somewhere near.

"I dodged behind some projecting rocks," said Mr. Stevens, "and my heart played like a trip hammer against my ribs. Finally I gathered myself up for a fine sprint. I ran as fast as I could over the rugged territory, the engineer and conductor of the train furnishing an escort.

"We reached Captain Polk's tent at Munroe's Camp and woke up the inmates. The safe was opened and the money transferred to it as expeditiously as possible. However I felt that I could not sleep, so Captain Polk and I sat up and chatted the balance of the night.

"From the tent the music and dancing at the Vinegaroon

Dance Hall could be plainly heard. This dance hall was in a very large tent pitched on a level place. Smooth rock formed the floor for the dancers. In fact Vinegaroon was all rock floored, the place being built, or pitched, on rocks.

"While we were conversing, someone came over from the dance hall and reported that two women had been shot. One of them had been killed outright. The other was badly wounded. The shooting was in the midst of a quadrille set. The dance was only stopped long enough to drag out the corpse of the dead woman and carry the wounded one to a neighboring tent.

"Besides the woman who was killed and the other one, who subsequently died from her wounds, another double tragedy took place in which two men bit the dust and died with their boots on.

"No, I did not visit the dance hall. I got all I wanted of it at long range."

In this sinful atmosphere Roy Bean not merely survived. He flourished. His tent saloon was a headquarters for gambling, drinking, and social gatherings. The rangers used his place as a hangout. And there wasn't much competition, for Roy knew how to dispose of competitors.

He used to tell how he ran one would-be rival out of business. As he was loafing around one morning, he noticed a carpenter just across the railroad tracks north of his saloon. The man was working busily and Roy, always suspicious of honest toil, went over and asked him what was going on.

"Putting up a saloon," said the carpenter.

"Who for?"

"That fellow over there."

The fellow in question, a Jewish gentleman, was tinkering with some boxes and barrels. Roy's suspicion grew darker. He strolled over and put his question once more.

"Sure he's putting up a saloon," said the second man. "For me."

"Well, you can't do it. I got here first."

"Oh yes, I can do it. I *am* doing it, ain't I?"

"Well, I can stop you."

"How do you think you can stop me?"

"I can do it. You wait and see."

Roy attended to business until the shack was finished. Then he sent a man over to see what was happening. The report was that "that Jew" was inside arranging his stock on his shelves.

"Watch me make a Jew leave the country," growled Roy. He got his Winchester rifle, filled the chamber, took aim, and shot a hole through the new saloon.

In a minute he fired again.

When the chamber was empty he refilled and started over. But long before the first load of cartridges was exhausted, the Jewish proprietor had emerged from the north side of his shack, the side away from danger, and moved toward Canada at a high rate of speed.

"What shall we do with his booze?" inquired Roy's roustabout after a brief inspection.

"Drink what you want," said Roy, magnanimously, "and bring the rest over here. I'll take care of it."

With such rough and ready tactics Roy enforced the "law," which was another name for his will. The effect was, on the whole, beneficial. Before long he was boasting to his visitors of the gentleness and harmony that had come to Vinegaroon.

"Everything is perfectly peaceful here," he would say. "The camp is as quiet as can be. There hasn't been a man killed for four hours."

LAW WEST OF THE PECOS

"LAW WEST OF THE PECOS" he called himself—and people thought he was joking. Law and order in that God-for-saken hell hole? Why half the badmen in Texas were on the dodge out there. A peace officer wouldn't last over-night in that climate, and what use would there be for a judge? Why hell, man, the United States Army couldn't clean it up!

"Maybe so," said Roy Bean. "Court will come to order. What's the charge, Sergeant?"

It was one of the first cases he handled, and a test of strength. Three crooked gamblers had got a stage-driver into a game and cleaned him out. After a run of bad luck like that the driver figured he could win if he had just a few more dollars. So he went out and sold the stage company's mules and then got into the game again.

Of course he lost, and there was a sudden interruption of stage accommodations to Vinegaroon. Time passed, and then one day the owner of the stage line arrived in town inquiring about his missing property. The matter wound up in Roy Bean's courtroom with the three gamblers up for trial for interfering with a public conveyance. Years later Judge Bean told his friend M. W. Tracy how it all came out.

"I ordered them to return the stage outfit and the money won," said he. "They got sore and as they were leaving they made some remarks that I didn't like.

" 'Bring those men back here,' I said. 'You are hereby fined thirty dollars apiece for gambling, and that ruling sticks.'

" 'You won't collect it!' says one of them, and they started out again. So I told the ranger to hang onto them and see that they stayed till the court was through with them.

" 'The fine is too high,' says the head gambler.

" 'How much did I say it was?'

" 'Thirty dollars.'

" 'Well, I guess I made a mistake. It is fifty dollars.'

"They howled like a bunch of coyotes, but I said, 'If I hear any more about it from you, it'll be a hundred dollars.'

"So they shut up and paid up."

Nobody laughed at Roy Bean's slogan after that. Later, when the Pecos River was saddled with iron bridges and the wild men were under ground or in Arizona, people forgot what it meant to be the Law West of the Pecos in 1882. They saw Roy Bean drunk in San Antonio, or butchering a goat at Langtry, and they said to themselves, "Why he's just an ordinary old soak." And some of them swaggered in front of him in their youth and ignorance until he short-changed them or arrested them. But the old-timers always speak respectfully of Roy's achievements at Vinegaroon. They have seen the rough times and the bad men, and they know what it took to bring any kind of law across the Pecos.

The lone justice was not completely on his own, for the handful of rangers backed him up, but it took some neat teamwork. One tale which is still told in many forms shows how they did it. This is the story about the time Roy almost hanged a lawyer. The old man gave his own

version to Joe Dwyer one afternoon over the beer bottles
in the tent at Vinegaroon.

The prisoner at the bar was as stubborn as a mule and
hated to let justice take its course. He had a lawyer with
him—a young squirt from Eagle Pass. The lawyer presented his credentials and Roy said, "Well, we'll try this
case whenever you are ready." So the trial began.

Every time Roy expressed a judicial opinion, the lawyer
would object. Then Roy would shake him off with,
"Objection overruled!"

Finally the lawyer got disgusted.

"I can see my client is not going to get justice in this
court. I am going to habeas corpus him."

"You're going to what?" inquired the Judge.

"Habeas corpus him."

"What does that mean?"

"Are you a justice of the peace and don't know what
a habeas corpus is? You ought to read the statutes."

"I have read 'em. Every word," and Roy laid his hand
on his famous law book.

The lawyer explained what he meant to do.

"Well, you can't do it," growled Roy. "I'll overrule
you."

The lawyer turned to a ranger sergeant standing by
with a couple of men. "This man can't behave in this
manner——"

"Listen!" interrupted Roy; then turned to the sergeant.
"Sergeant."

"Yes, sir."

"What are your orders here?"

"To stand behind you in everything you say."

"What would you do if I told you to take this fellow out
and hang him?"

"I'd take him out and hang him."

"Oh," gasped the lawyer, "you couldn't do that!"

"Well, I will! And furthermore I won't even take you out in this hot sun to hang you. I'll hang you to the ridge pole right here in the saloon."

The lawyer pondered very briefly. Then wisdom descended upon him.

"I think I'll drop the case," he said.

Once out of the neighborhood, he decided to carry the matter to Austin, as Roy usually told the story, and went directly to the governor. The governor refused to take any action. "Those boys are running the show out there," he said. "Let them run it!"

He was right. The boys were running the show and running it wide open. Howls of rage and groans of protest went up into the clear trans-Pecos air from the drunks and tin horns and gun slingers. Rumors of strange and irregular proceedings reached the ears of county and district authorities. Finally District Judge T. A. Falvey of El Paso was appealed to and he set out for Vinegaroon to see about it. The railroad which was building east from El Paso was still many miles from the Pecos. Judge Falvey went as far as he could by train and then took a buggy to make the last stage. He arrived while Roy was trying a misdemeanor case in his combination barroom and court of justice. A newspaper reporter many years later got the story from Mr. Falvey himself.

"Just as Judge Falvey entered the canvas courtroom the jury, which had been deliberating on the fate of the accused, returned with the report that they could not reach a decision. At the off hip of the presiding dignitary was a pearl-handled six-shooter, the El Paso attorney said. He deliberately pulled the gun and laid it carefully in front of him on the table. Addressing the jury, he told them that hung juries might be all right in some communities but it would not go in his court. He then sent the jury back into the rear of the tent to deliberate further with the threat that they would be chained to the post outside of the tent which served the grizzled old justice as a jail. The verdict was immediately rendered against the defendant."

That may seem like pretty high-handed procedure but it worked out all right—in fact it worked out much better than a good many examples of legal practice today in which smart lawyers find ways of delaying and obstructing justice at the public expense.

Roy Bean couldn't afford to have such things happen in his jurisdiction. Supposing a case had to be carried on up to the courts at Fort Stockton. A ranger would have to accompany the prisoner on the two-hundred-mile journey. That would leave one less officer to handle the turbulent mob in the Vinegaroon gin mills. Furthermore it was as hard to get witnesses over to Fort Stockton as it was to transport the prisoners. And finally it cost money. It seemed best to Roy Bean and the rangers to handle their business on the spot. So they handled it. And as the railroad operations approached their finish and the two ends of track drew closer, there was more business to handle.

The horse-thief story shows how this rugged frontier justice operated. One day a rancher brought in a sorry-looking specimen and lined him up before the Judge.

"What's he charged with?"

"Stealing horses, Judge."

"Whose horses?"

"Mine."

"You sure about it?"

"Caught him at it. He was drawing them across the ford."

"Who nicked his ear?"

"I did when he didn't stop."

"Too bad you're such a damn poor shot."

Judge Bean thereupon took the man's gun away and advised him with deep earnestness, "Now you get the hell out of here and if you're ever caught in these parts again you'll be strung up pronto."

The horse thief disappeared down the track and as far as Roy was concerned justice had been done. The horses had been recovered. The thief had a good chance of getting back to civilization, though his lack of horse and gun complicated his problem considerably. At least the man was gone; the county had no expense over him; and the ranger force was still intact. Maybe it wasn't good law but it was good common sense.

There was common sense behind most of Roy's decisions, even the ones which at first seem most eccentric. And he probably knew a little law. His one and only law book, the Revised Statutes of Texas for 1879 (still preserved at Langtry), was up to date when he got it and he thumbed it thoroughly. Some pages are dog-eared and even pencil-marked—the section specifying how much land the railroad may reserve for right of way, the clauses of the penal code relating to cattle stealing and similar offenses. On the back fly leaf is written in Roy's crabbed hand "10 bottles to Jesus," which indicates that the volume was useful in his rude bookkeeping as well as in his court of law. Probably he didn't consult it often, and he certainly never made any effort to keep abreast of new legislation. "Yes, they send me a new book every year or so," he said once; "but I use it to light fires with."

His seat of justice in those times was much inferior to the more elegant and expensive frame building which he built at Langtry in later days, but even at Vinegaroon he managed to make himself comfortable. Judge Bean was never one to put up with unnecessary physical hardships, though he didn't ask for rugs and curtains and modern plumbing. Jess Fry, who held the post of telegraph operator at Vinegaroon, used to describe Roy's arrangements. First there was his law book. Then there was a chair on which the Judge sat to deal monte and dispense justice. The law book rested on the chair and the Judge rested on the law book, his elbows on the table which held the monte layout. Thus, said Mr. Fry, "all he had to do was to move the monte layout to one side, take the book out from under him, and proceed with the 'case.' "

When a jury was required, the men sat on barrels and boxes in front of the Judge and recesses were frequent during which Roy transformed himself into a bartender. Everybody was supposed to drink—judge, jury, prisoner, and all. In later years he used his courts to stimulate business about as much as to dispense justice. But in his Vinegaroon days he tended to his knitting.

The prisoners had to put up with even cruder accommodations than Roy's own. There was a gnarled stump of a tree in front of his tent—they say it was the only one in the country—and anybody who had to be detained was chained to that trunk. This idea was not original with Roy. The rangers were in the habit of making a man embrace a tree before slipping the handcuffs on him when they wanted him to stay in one place for a while.

Any of Roy's friends who happened to get picked up were not, of course, required to put up with such confinement. For them he found loopholes in the regulations which an ordinary man of law would never have thought of. For instance there was the young fellow who was arrested for carrying concealed weapons.

"The charge won't stick," pronounced Judge Bean. "If he was standing still when he was arrested he wasn't carrying weapons because he wasn't going no place. And if he was not standing still he was traveling, and it's legal for travelers to carry weapons. Case dismissed."

Prisoners and bystanders alike were impressed by Roy's methods. Having been in and out of law courts all his life, he had a fluent command of a jargon that sounded like the best legal language. His overbearing manner, his booming voice, and his glittering eye cowed the toughest offenders. The Law West of the Pecos put on a good show.

At least at first he carried out his duties (as he saw them) conscientiously. He even made returns to the Commissioners' Court at Fort Stockton. Anyway he did once. That was on November 16, 1883. The Commissioners' Minutes read:

The Report of Roy Bean Justice of the Peace showing amount of Fines collected to be $89.00 By receipt of Sheriff to be $36.65. Express insured to be $35.00 and the balance due Pecos county to be $17.35—was read and approved by order of the court.

It is often said that Roy Bean always pocketed his fines, declaring that his court had to be self-sustaining. No doubt he kept most of his collections, but this once at least he did right by the county authorities, even though the sheriff had to collect the first installment of what was owed and the account was still in arrears when the report was approved.

DEFEAT AT STRAWBRIDGE

IN THE COURSE of his long and sinful career Roy Bean had spent a good share of his time trying to get something for nothing from somebody who had a better right to it than he had. Thanks to his craft and his skill at the great game of bluff, he had a long string of victories to his credit; and on the few occasions when the battle had gone against him, he usually considered that he had won a sort of immoral victory. Now it was his turn to take a first-class licking with no possible alibis.

The curtain goes up on the interior of the tent saloon at Vinegaroon. Time: December of 1882. Roy Bean is alone in his establishment. He stands in the middle of the litter of papers and packing straw which usually decorates his floor and gazes gloomily into the cash box. He combs his thick, iron-gray beard with his fingers and seems submerged in cheerless thoughts.

A sunburned young roughneck in overalls thrusts his head inside the tent and shouts joyfully, "Goodbye, Roy! See you in Santone."

"What the hell are you going to Santone for?" inquires Roy sourly.

"Got laid off this morning. Won't be anything here much longer and they'll be giving this hell hole back to the buzzards. Better pack up and come along."

With a bilious look and a disgusted grunt Roy turns away.

Something like this must have happened, for at the end of 1882 Vinegaroon began to fold up. The contractors were shipping their equipment out. A steady trickle of men flowed back to San Antonio. Only a feeble silver tinkle was heard in the cash box which had once echoed to the rich, melodious crackle of greenbacks. Roy was sensitive to those changes—particularly to those in the pitch and volume of his money—and he began to ask himself, "What next?"

There was no question of returning to San Antonio. Back there he was just a crooked, thirsty, poverty-stricken old scoundrel from Beanville. Out here he was the Law West of the Pecos. There was only one choice possible for a man with Roy's ego—he would stay in West Texas.

So he kept his ear to the ground and at last got news of a place where his talents might be useful. This was the town of Strawbridge (now called Sanderson), named for a top-notch construction engineer and soon to become a division point on the new railroad. It was a moderately lively place located among the barren hills seventy-odd miles west of Vinegaroon. It was supposed to be short on law and beer, so Roy Bean regretfully said farewell to the place where for the first time in his life he had been a public benefactor, loaded his highly portable equipment on a wagon, and headed west for the last time. Late in 1882 Strawbridge awoke one morning to find that Roy Bean was its newest citizen.

This news was especially interesting to a man named Charlie Wilson who had been the newest citizen just a few days before and was already carrying on a lively saloon business. Charlie was a big Irishman with a sense of humor and a way of getting things done. Eventually he came to own most of Sanderson, but in those days he was just getting started and was known mostly for his oversize hands which seemed to be especially made for wrapping themselves about a deck of cards and completely concealing what was happening to the kings and jacks.

Roy and Charlie knew each other, at least by reputation, and were aware that the town wasn't big enough to hold both of them. Roy's technique in such cases was to sit tight while he wore the other fellow down or scared him off. Wilson, however, had a little more imagination and went to work in secret ways to rid himself of the Bean menace.

First he bought up the best business locations so as to make it hard for a rival to get started. Then he put on the pressure. In the deepest shades of midnight, when all Strawbridge was sleeping soundly, a Mexican in Wilson's pay approached the Bean saloon on cat feet. He had a large tin can in his hand. Stealthily he stole inside, spent thirty seconds at the whiskey barrel, and oozed out again without a sound, while the owner of the barrel snored on unsuspectingly.

In the morning Roy opened up as usual and served a snort of Hill & Hill to an early customer. The man swallowed blissfully; then opened his eyes wide, made a nasty face, coughed, swore, and left indignantly. The next two drinkers followed his example. Then Roy sampled the whiskey himself and found it strongly flavored with kerosene. Within a very few hours he had loaded up his possessions and headed back for the Pecos. He knew he had been outheld and it was time to quit the game.

Neither of the men ever talked much about the incident Wilson couldn't be persuaded to admit, even by his best friends, that he was responsible for the kerosene in the whiskey barrel. All Roy would ever say in explanation of his return to the Pecos country was this revealing sentence:

"I came back because I wanted to live where I could tell 'em what to do."

Roy and Charlie saw each other off and on after that and seem to have kept up a humorous antagonism. Some years after Roy's sudden departure a couple of young bulls belonging to Wilson got loose and wandered as far as Langtry where they were impounded in the Bean corral. Wilson heard where they were and came down to claim them.

"Roy, I've come after those bulls."

"Well, that's all right, but you'll have to pay some damages."

"What damages? I don't see any fields around here or crops they could have damaged, and there ain't a fence for a hundred miles."

"No, but I had some virgin heifers here, and your bulls seduced 'em."

Wilson paid off, expecting to get Roy into a poker game later and even the score. He probably did, though neither Wilson nor Roy mentioned the matter when they referred to it in later years.

It was getting close to Christmas when the retreat was completed. Roy got down off his wagon and looked around on familiar scenes. He was about to make camp at Eagle's Nest, the place where he had begun his career west of the Pecos. A small boom seemed to be on the make in that neighborhood. Men were lining up the rails on the new road bed and a water tank was under construction a few hundred yards west of the water hole. Everybody was talking about the ceremonies which were to mark the joining of the ends of track in Dead Man's

Canyon. Around the water tank a town site was being laid out by Jesus P. Torres, whose father owned the land. Roy's cunning eye took in the situation and schemes began to form in his shaggy head.

Meanwhile the days went by and on January 12, 1883, the tracks were joined with much ceremony. Colonel Pierce came in his private car from the east. Collis P. Huntington came in his private car from the west. There was a silver (some say gold) spike involved, along with a California redwood tie, and you would never have known that the railroad magnates had been trying to cut each other's throats a few weeks before.

Roy used to tell how he made a dash after that silver spike as soon as the coast was clear, but a bigger operator than he had got there first. Colonel Pierce had taken the spike away as a souvenir. Even the redwood tie was cut up into small pieces and distributed among the official guests.

As Roy looked at the place where the silver spike should have been, he realized that the boom days were done—the days of wild and lawless construction camps, of waves of humanity washing into the saloons and cemeteries. But the railroad was there and trains would run from New Orleans to San Francisco. Engines would have to stop for water. Passengers would be hungry and thirsty. Roy looked up at the water tank on the slope above the old camp at Eagle's Nest and made up his mind. That would be his town. There he could "tell 'em what to do."

VICTORY AT LANGTRY

THE FACT IS, Roy had no business settling down in the new and nameless town beside that water tank. Nobody wanted him there and he had no legal hold on a square inch of the barren, rocky land. Yet through sheer brazen impertinence he made the place his own and rode herd on it for twenty years.

The story of this triumph of effrontery is the history of Bean's feud with Jesus P. Torres—a feud which smoldered until Bean was too old to squabble any more and which might have flared up any time if Torres had not been pretty cautious.

No doubt there was some personal dislike mixed up in their troubles, but the root of the matter was that they got in each other's way. Both of them wanted to run the town and both of them wanted to monopolize the beer business. From their respective bases in the Jersey Lily on the north side of the tracks and in the Eagle's Nest saloon on the south side of the tracks they carried on guerrilla operations against each other for many years.

Torres was a better man than the Roy Bean stories give him credit for being. He was a big, handsome Mexican—well educated for those times, very much of a gentleman, and married to a woman of German ancestry. His chief trouble was that he did not like to fight, and this fact Roy was not long in discovering. By bringing into play his natural talents as a bluffer, he usually came out on top—though not always.

What made it worse for Torres was the fact that he had counted on being the big man of the new town and had every reason for feeling that he should be. His father, Cesario Torres, was a rich old Mexican cattle baron who had developed the great 7D cattle ranch higher up the Pecos and had acquired title to much additional property including the land which surrounded the new water tank. Thus Jesus P. Torres, the son, really and literally owned the town; and when Roy moved his tent up the hill to the new location, there wasn't any place where he could legally set up his business.

He solved the problem by squatting on the railroad right of way, probably edging over onto Torres' property. Torres minded this much more than the railroad did, for the Southern Pacific never forgot Roy's early exploits in pacifying Vinegaroon. Roy in his turn labored to deserve the favors that came his way. When the town was in the process of birth there were some special difficulties that put him to the test. Torres owned Pump Canyon, on the outskirts of town, which contained the only supply of good water in the neighborhood, and it took Roy Bean to persuade him to hand this property over to the railroad. Whether Roy used bribery, seduction, or threats, it is impossible now to tell, but he wasn't ordinarily given to bribery or seduction. From that time on the Southern Pacific granted him an annual pass; usually he forgot to carry it, though he rode free anyhow.

Torres naturally resented all this interference with his hopes and plans, but what could he do? Bean was always two jumps ahead of him. If only the pest could be got rid of entirely! Wait! Now he had it! Maybe there was a way after all.

Torres' idea was a pretty good one. He had already

agreed to turn over half the lots in his new townsite to the railroad and in return the company was to erect a station around which a village would naturally grow. When it was time to close the deal, however, Torres added a clause (so says Ruel McDaniel in his little book *Vinegarroon*) stipulating that Roy Bean might never buy any of the land Torres gave up.

The Southern Pacific agreed to this arrangement and Torres felt better than he had for months.

But Roy had learned in San Antonio how not to be ejected from places where he didn't belong, and the Jersey Lily kept on doing a land-office business south of the tracks for several years in spite of hell, high water, and Jesus P. Torres. It is usually said that one of his friends was persuaded to buy a lot from Torres and then transfer the title to Bean. However Roy did it, he managed to sit tight and soon built up a thriving business in the small frame building which housed himself, his whiskey barrel, and his four children whom he brought out from San Antonio as soon as he had a place to put them.

About 1888 he moved to roomier quarters north of the tracks, again double-crossing poor Señor Torres. The railroad helped. The officials kept to the letter of their agreement with Torres but neatly sidestepped the spirit. How they did it is revealed in an extraordinary document which became a part of the deed record of Val Verde County on April 24, 1888. It reads:

This agreement made and entered into this day by and between Roy Bean of said county and state and the Galveston Harrisburg and San Antonio Railway by C. C. Gibbs Land Commissioner; witnesseth, that the said Railway Company this day leases to Roy Bean Lot eighteen in Block fifteen in the town of Langtry as shown by the map thereof for and until the termination of the lease of the United States now held by C. Torres on a part of the said town when the said lease of the United States is terminated and then the said Railway Company hereby agrees to convey to Samuel Bean son of Roy Bean Lot number ten in Block number twenty-one in the said town of Langtry as shown by the map thereof. The said lot is to be deeded to Samuel Bean without cost to him, and said Roy Bean agrees to move his place of business from where it now stands on and to Lot Eighteen in Block Fifteen until the Deed above named can be obtained and said Roy Bean is hereby permitted to put his house temporarily at the east of the right-of-way until the deed aforesaid is delivered said removal to be made as soon as practicable with privilege of buying the lot "of land" on which his house is "to be" built for 50.00 signed in San Antonio this 24 day of April 1888.

In other words, the Southern Pacific allowed him to continue with its blessing to squat on the right of way until the officials could lease him (not sell him) one of their lots. Later on Roy could either buy the lot he had leased or move onto Sam's lot.

Nobody can say now just why the agreement was drawn in this mysterious fashion but it shows how a great corporation paid its debts in the dear dead days beyond recall.

For twenty years the Bean-Torres feud smoldered, flaring up occasionally and scattering sparks over the bystanders. A typical tale is told of the time that Torres was holding open house at his joint across the tracks. All present were having a high old time. The noise at last became so loud as the cowboys, rustlers, sheepmen, and smugglers took on more liquor that Roy decided to interfere. He sent Phil Forrest, his constable, over to the

Eagle's Nest and had him arrest Torres for disturbing the peace.

Next day Torres grumbled about the interference with his business and surmised (aloud) that the Judge was sore because Torres was getting all the trade.

This remark was peddled around until it reached Roy, who thereupon took down his Winchester, loaded it, and told one of his Mexicans to go over and inform Torres that he was going to get him the first time he stuck his head out of the door.

Torres got the message and cocked an eye around the door jamb. There was Roy on his porch, rifle across his knees, ready for business.

Soon a white rag on a stick was thrust out of Torres' doorway, waved vigorously, and then followed by Torres himself. He approached the enemy stronghold gingerly and inquired, "What's the trouble about? Why do you want to shoot me this time?"

"You said I arrested you because you were corralling all the business," replied Roy, "and I'm going to blow your goddam head off!"

"It's a lie!" yelled Torres. "I never said it!"

But Roy made him swear it on the cross before the rifle was unloaded and put away—at least so runs the tale.

Some time later (says rumor) Torres was arrested again, this time on a charge of assault. He probably never assaulted anybody in his life, but let's not spoil the story. Haled before Judge Bean, Torres found himself in the presence not merely of a judge but of a jury as well. Twelve good men, tried, true, and thirsty, were to judge him. The trial lasted for some time and the good men grew thirstier. When it was their turn to speak they brought in a verdict of guilty and recommended that the accused be fined two dozen bottles of beer. Torres was delighted to get off so easily. "All right, boys," he said, rubbing his hands together joyfully, "come right over to my saloon and get your beer."

"Oh, no, you don't!" cut in Judge Bean. "The jury's decision is all right with me, but the fines imposed in this here court are paid on the spot, and don't you forget it!"

So Torres had to pay the retail price for two dozen bottles of beer.

An especially interesting angle of the feud came in with the second generation. In the mid-nineties Roy's son Sam was in his romantic twenties and ripe for romance. It came in the person of Mrs. Torres' younger sister who was of an age and appearance to upset a Bean's emotional balance. She was plump, she was pretty, and she seemed to like Sam.

Of course an orthodox friendship was impossible. Mrs. Torres knew of the situation and sympathized. So did the neighbors. But they were all afraid Torres might do some mischief to Sam if he found out, and in that case Roy would certainly do a mischief to Torres. Consequently Sam and his little German girl were unable to develop anything more than a smiling acquaintance while the situation lasted.

It lasted only a short time. Sam didn't care for too much concentration in matters of this kind, and the old-timers say that when the next new face appeared in Langtry he was off in pursuit at once, thus spoiling a good tragedy in the first act.

The decisive skirmish in the battle between the two rivals was really the first one. It takes us back to the time when the town was named. It should probably have been

© N. H. Rose

Roy Bean and his family
From left to right: Zulema, Little Roy, Roy, Sam, and Laura

The Law West of the Pecos

© N. H. Rose

Judge Bean on old Bayo

© N. H. Rose

Morning mood at the Jersey Lily

The only known picture of the old saloon, destroyed by fire in 1899

The Jersey Lily falling to pieces after Roy Bean's death

Fitzsimmons-Maher fight; the bridge over the Rio Grande

The Ring and a few of the spectators

Mrs. Langtry

called Ciudad Torres or Torres Center or something like that. Instead it became Langtry.

At the time the famous English actress Lily Langtry, friend of the Prince of Wales and toast of European society, was bearing all before her on her first American tour. Audiences were wild with admiration of her clothes, her figure, and (in rare cases) of her acting. American men were reduced to lumps of quivering jelly when she cast her eyes upon them. Every detail of her life and personality was considered front-page news and Americans everywhere felt a solemn thrill on learning that Mrs. Langtry was very fond of oysters.

Naturally Roy had heard of the Jersey Lily, and the stories all say that he had found a picture of her to admire before he ever came within a thousand miles of her. After one look at those lovely features (and they were lovely), old Roy Bean, nearing sixty and as rough and tough as they came, felt a gentle, spring-like stirring in his battered breast. Love he had known in many shades and degrees but this was something different. It was the breathless feeling Dante had for Beatrice—what poetry calls "the desire of the moth for the star." And it was the real and permanent thing. His friends all testify that whenever he spoke of her, from the picture episode on, it was with a voice and a look of worship. And nobody laughed at him for it, either.

Now Roy was a man of action and not the type to sit back and twiddle his sensations. When he was smitten by the fist of man or the eye of woman he had to do something about it. In this case he felt a need to make sacrifice at the altar of his devotion—offer something precious to his goddess—make her aware of his existence. The first thing his fellow townsmen knew there was a sign over his door

advising them that henceforth they would do their drinking in the JERSEY LILLY.

Still he wasn't satisfied. Her name was written over
his door but not among the stars, and he needed to make his
gesture more magnificent. Before long he figured out a
solution—he would give her the whole blasted town, or
at least put her brand on it. That was the answer! He
would christen the place Langtry.

Roy must have made this decision almost as soon as the
town was laid out. Mrs. Langtry says in her reminiscences
that she received a letter from him telling of the naming
of "her town" during her second year in the States. She
arrived in New York in the fall of 1882. Hence the letter
probably reached her in the winter of 1883–84 and it may
well be that she was the first one notified. Anyway on
December 8, 1884, before Torres knew what was happening, the Post Office Department made the name official,
legal, and permanent.

Mrs. Langtry had never had a town named after her
before, though she was used to having babies, hats, and
other miscellaneous objects titled in her honor. Naturally
she was deeply touched and in her turn cast about for a
suitable gesture to show her feelings. Roy had urged
her to pay the place a visit. "It was at that moment
impossible," she says, "and on writing him my regrets, I
offered to present an ornamental drinking fountain as a
sop; but Roy Bean's quick reply was that it would be
quite useless, as the only thing the citizens of Langtry
did *not* drink was water."

Many years passed before the great lady was able to pay
her town a visit, but nothing could change the feelings of
her devoted admirer out west of the Pecos. He displayed
her picture prominently on the wall of his barroom and

often pointed to it proudly. "That," he would say, "is who this town is named after."

It is still possible to start a fight in Texas over the naming of Langtry. The railroad officials will tell you today that the community took its title from a construction foreman who helped to run the line through the Pecos country and that the Jersey Lily had nothing to do with it. There is a possibility that the officials are right, but Roy Bean never had the beginning of a suspicion that anybody but himself and Lily Langtry were concerned. Furthermore all the surviving old-timers and the present-day citizens of Langtry take it for granted that he was right.

At least the town was named without the knowledge and consent of Jesus P. Torres, though it was his private property.

PUBLIC SERVANT

Roy Bean got most of his leverage at Langtry from his official dignity as a justice. Shorn of that, he was shorn of his power and glory, and naturally he took all precautions to avoid the shears. At first it was easy; later it wasn't. His original appointment in 1882 gave him two sweet years of authority and he had no difficulty in getting himself legally elected in 1884—partly, perhaps, because his house was the official voting place for the precinct. Then things began to happen. In 1885 the politicians formed a new county (Val Verde) in the Pecos and Devil's River area, and Roy found himself with new horizons. His county seat was now Del Rio, and the great reaches to the westward were no longer part of his domain.

He had an uncomfortable feeling that civilization was moving in on him and that he was no longer "all the law west of the Pecos." It was hard to take. In fact he didn't take it without a struggle and tried his best to ignore such flimsy, man-made barriers as county lines.

A train wreck gave him a chance to show how he felt. It occurred at Eldridge, many miles west of Langtry and in Pecos County. Cause of the trouble was the carelessness of a brakeman who stepped off a freight train at Dryden and was somehow left behind. The engineer pulled on to Eldridge where he was supposed to side-track while a passenger train went by. The brakeman should have closed

the switch but was not on hand to do his duty. The passenger train came along, plowed into the rear of the
freight, and killed the passenger engineer.

Roy heard of the tragedy and hot-footed it up to
Eldridge to hold an inquest (an inquest was worth five
dollars to the official who performed it). After taking
careful note of the evidence, he found the negligent brakeman guilty of murder for not closing the switch. Then,
learning that the engineer of the passenger train had
neglected to blow his whistle on approaching the siding,
he found him an accessory after the fact to his own death.

It is not known whether or not he collected his five
dollars for this masterly ruling.

The next rub in his official career was the election of
1886. In that year a man named John Gilcrease ran against
him and won, twenty-five votes to seventeen. Gilcrease
was a hardy West Texan who dug wells and did odd
jobs for the railroad. He wasn't serious about becoming
an office holder at first—probably he just wanted to make
old Roy sweat a little. Then when the votes began to
pile up, he saw the advantages of being a judge. After
the election he made his bond, hung out a shingle, and
even performed an inquest on the body of one Vincent
Gonzales, for which he collected the usual five dollars
from the county commissioners.

No doubt Roy heard of that five dollars which should
have been in his pocket. He certainly got busy and pulled
some wires, for on February 18, 1887, the Commissioners'
Court took extraordinary measures to see that Roy got
what was coming to him. They established a new Justice
Court Precinct embracing all of Val Verde County west
of the Pecos River and then ordered "that Roy Bean be
and is hereby appointed Justice of the Peace in and for

precinct no. 5 and that he give bond and qualify as the law directs." They also established a new road precinct with the same boundaries as the justice precinct and appointed Roy road overseer (he was in the habit of putting his prisoners to work on the roads). And so he was still Law West of the Pecos—in reduced form.

How well he carried on the war is revealed again in the Commissioners' minutes. On May 11, 1887, John Gilcrease appeared in court and resigned his commission. On the same day Roy Bean appeared to qualify for his own office. It looks as if they had made a deal of some kind and had come up to Del Rio together to put it through.

In a chat with his old California friend, Major Horace Bell, Roy gave his version of what happened:

"One time as an election approached some boosters for another settlement that had sprung up down nearer the river put up a rival candidate to Roy. The latter feeling so sure that his reelection was automatically assured, gave little attention to the rival claimant, with the result that the upstart was actually elected and the judicial seat moved down to the river bank.

" 'But I am the only man that could ever make anything out of the office,' said Justice Bean to me when he was laughing about that political slip up, 'and in a little while the Rio Grande judge came up to propose to me that I buy him out. He brought his commission along with him, his docket and all his papers, and dickered with me. He was sick of the job. So I gave him a demijohn of whiskey, two bear skins and a pet coon for the right, title, honor, and emoluments of the office!' "

Warned by this lesson, Roy looked to his political fences thereafter, winning the election in 1888 and 1890.

In 1892 he ran against a snag in the form of Lon Tatum, a good-natured Langtryite with a refined taste in whiskey who was put up for the office by a pair of cattle-raising brothers named Reagan. They electioneered so success- fully that they threw a scare into Roy and he appealed to his friends on the railroad to help. They were willing to do their best, and soon a work train was shunted off on the Langtry siding with thirty or forty men aboard who immediately became, in good old Texas fashion, legal residents qualified to vote. Next day was election day and everyone performed his patriotic duty. In fact most of those present voted twice. When a burro lifted his voice on the hill behind the saloon, they even pressed him into service, placing a marked ballot between his teeth and shoving his head through the window to the ballot box with another vote for Roy Bean.

The Reagan brothers had been set back on their heels by the arrival of the work train but, recovering rapidly, they began to use persuasion on the new citizens and won many of them over. "We mixed with those bridge men," says Lee Reagan, a cousin who was present, "knew some anyway, and persuaded them not to block us, and most of them voted with us and the judge was beaten badly, and what do you think he did—he said once a justice always a justice, and went on and held his courts, and our friend Tatum never got any action nor qualified, nor knew what to do about it I guess."

This does not agree with county records which state that in the election of November 7, 1892, Roy Bean got forty-one votes and Lon Tatum got fifteen. That might or might not mean anything. About all anyone can be sure of is that there was bound to be something peculiar about an election in Langtry in those days; and no matter who won, Roy would continue to function as justice of the peace.

In the next election (1894) Roy was unopposed, but when November of 1896 rolled around, there was more funny business than ever before and the Bean-Torres feud was revived to add spice to the situation. By now the town was at the peak of its prosperity and Judge Bean's influence was not so strong as formerly, so J. P. Torres decided to run against the old man.

As soon as Torres announced, Roy flew into a lather of activity. He electioneered, fumed, threatened, and took precautions which seemingly made it impossible for him to lose. When the ballots were counted he had considerably more votes (some say a hundred) than the number of qualified voters in the precinct. As a result the vote was "thrown out" by the Commissioners and J. P. Torres was appointed to serve in Roy's stead.

It nearly broke his heart. Not to be "the Judge" was, in his view, not to be anything. He couldn't bear to think of it. So when Torres sent an underling over to the Jersey Lily to demand the seal and law book, Roy refused point blank to deliver them and told the messenger to get the hell out of there.

All the demands of Torres and all the commands of the county authorities were useless, and eventually it became customary, if not legal, for Roy to try all the cases that came up on the north side of the track while Torres handled those on the south side—if he got there first.

In 1898 Roy and Torres again opposed each other and again Roy overreached himself. The election was held in the little schoolhouse on the hill behind the Jersey Lily, and before it was well under way Roy was patrolling a beat in front of the schoolhouse door with his sawed-off shotgun in the crook of his arm. All who came to the polls had to submit to questioning as to their political views, and anybody who looked like a Torres supporter was sent away with threats and insults.

Somebody telegraphed the authorities at Del Rio and Sheriff Almonds boarded a train and came up.

"Well, Roy," he said, "I hear you're not letting these people vote."

"By God, I won't let 'em if they vote the wrong way."

The sheriff pointed to Roy's pet bear chained near the saloon.

"I'm going to handcuff you to that bear if you keep on." And he got out his handcuffs.

Roy saw that the game was up. "You've got the gun," he said sadly. "I guess I'll have to let 'em vote."

Torres won, twenty-six votes to fifteen.

That was Torres' last shot, however. In 1900 he ran again but got only ten votes to Roy's 19. In 1902, the last time he ever ran, Roy was unopposed. When he died a year and a half later he was still Law West of the Pecos.

They carved those words on his tombstone; and if they hadn't he would have climbed out of his grave and done something about it.

MARRIAGE BROKER

THE ROY BEAN LEGEND got started early. Stories of strange but sensible decisions and of original contributions to the law of the land were in circulation almost as soon as the Judge settled down at Langtry. There was apparently no sort of difficulty he did not feel able to handle. For instance, there was the matter of divorce.

It seems that Roy very soon became a sort of little father to the poor Mexican families in his neighborhood. He fed them, bullied them, fined them, cursed them, and interfered in their private affairs when he thought it necessary. They stood in great awe of him and he enjoyed playing God among them.

Early in Bean's career at Langtry, Joe Dwyer stopped by on his way to San Antonio and found two Mexican track workers in the saloon with their wives. They were *pobrecitos*, living in box cars and pretty close to the primitive in their notions about life. Each couple wanted to be divorced. The Judge obliged them and collected two dollars apiece. With many thanks they bowed themselves out of the courtroom and started away—one couple in one direction, one in the other. Roy observed that they had exchanged partners and he smelled a rat.

So he called them back.

"Here, you can't go off together that way. You can't live together without getting married. I'll have to arrest you for fornication."

They talked it over in a flurry of Spanish words and gestures and reached a decision.

"All right," said one. "How much will it cost?"

"Five dollars apiece."

Another consultation ended in the counting of money. They had enough. The Judge married each man to the other's ex-wife and that was that.

The rumor went around that Roy Bean's marriage mill was now working in reverse and those who knew the law said severe things about such proceedings. Roy himself began to worry about it and decided to ask for some advice. In a day or two Lawyer John M. Dean of El Paso went through on his way to Austin and Roy buttonholed him as the train paused to take on water.

"Mr. Dean, I want to ask you about a p'int of law."

"Go ahead, Roy."

"Well, I just divorced two couples and married each of the women to the other man. I want to know if it was legal."

Mr. Dean was willing to let Judge Bean handle his own affairs. "Well, you did it, didn't you?" he said. "I guess it'll have to be legal."

Somewhat reassured, Roy went back to the Jersey Lily and relaxed; but in a very few days he had to start worrying again. High officials began dropping in to inquire about the rumor that he was granting divorces. Roy told a man from the San Antonio *Light* about the first one:

"It was not long after this that a certain judge got wind of the proceedings and called on me at Langtry. He told me I had exceeded my authority, and that he would be compelled to arrest me and take me to the jail at Ft. Stockton. I finally succeeded in getting the judge to remain overnight in Langtry, and knowing he was fond of playing poker, I sent out for some of the boys.

"The judge had about twenty dollars with him which he soon lost. Of course I supplied him with money from time to time, and when daylight came the judge owed me about five hundred dollars.

"He called for his horse and rode away without mentioning anything more about the criminal proceedings against me for granting the divorce, and I did not remind him of the money he had borrowed from me. After he was gone, the boys came around and gave me my money back."

By this time District Judge Falvey of El Paso had got wind of the affair and to Roy's embarrassment he too came down to Langtry with the usual question on his lips. Roy was getting a little tired of it, and although he usually had profound respect for a real, honest-to-God Judge like Mr. Falvey, he decided to stand his ground.

"Divorces can be granted only in the district court," said Judge Falvey, very seriously.

"Well," Roy objected stubbornly, "I married 'em, didn't I?"

"Yes, I hear you did."

"Then I guess I got a right to unmarry 'em if it didn't take. The way I figure it, I was just rectifyin' an error and a man's got a right to do that."

And in spite of Judge Falvey's remarks about what would happen if the performance were repeated, Roy refused to change his mind. In fact, he did it again in 1893 or 1894 and men are still to be found who saw it happen. H. L. Howell was living at Langtry in those days, and had watched for some time a strange quirk of human nature. Two married Mexicans were making up to each other's wives; and although one was just as guilty as the other, they were both feeling very resentful about their tarnished family honor. It looked as if there might be a killing.

At this point Judge Bean stepped forward, herded them in, divorced them, shuffled them up, and remarried them. Then he put a ranger in charge of each couple to prevent fireworks, and had one sent east on the next train while the other went west. Neither couple was ever heard from again and Roy told himself that he had done a good day's work for suffering humanity. Besides, he had collected a fat fee.

A third case occurred in 1901 or 1902, a couple of years before Judge Bean passed on to a larger courtroom. The late W. D. Greet of El Paso was there and used to laugh about how the problem was complicated by the long line of offspring which followed each couple to the bar of justice. That night the old man appeared at Mrs. Dodd's boarding house for supper, looking very tired. "Judge," said Mrs. Dodd, "you look all in. What's been happening to you?"

"Well, I am tired. I divorced two couples this afternoon, swapped 'em around, and remarried them. Then I spent the rest of the day dividing up the children."

When a friend quizzed him on the streets of El Paso one time about his divorces, he slapped his pocket significantly and said with a wink, "If they won't team up let 'em carry single."

To tell the honest truth, the marrying business, with or without the privilege of cancellation or exchange, added a nice percentage to Judge Bean's income. He performed marriages for Mexicans and Americans alike, and he would do the job anywhere it needed to be done. He probably enjoyed his Mexican marriages most. Sometimes he held them in his saloon and sometimes in the schoolhouse.

Usually he would be pretty well lubricated when it was time to begin and in a mood to prolong the ceremony half the night. Frequently he would put the bride and groom through various complicated evolutions such as promenading round and round the hall while he thought up something else to say or do. The climax would come something like this:

"Both of you hold up your right hands."

The couple would obey.

"By the authority of the Constitution of the United States, the great State of Texas, and the Law West of the Pecos, I, Roy Bean, Justice of the Peace of this district, hereby pronounce you man and wife. May God have mercy on your souls."

A wedding was usually a five-dollar affair, though sometimes collections were slow. H. L. Howell tells of the time when a Mexican Indian about four and a half feet high and short on intelligence came up to the saloon to be married. There he stood, hat in both hands, the color of a well-weathered saddle, his woman just about as short and as black.

The Judge knew the couple well, knew they had been living together, and wondered why they wished to get married at this late stage of affairs.

"Well," said the Indian, "I thought it would be better Also our friends say we ought to."

So Roy married them and then said, "*Cinco pesos.*"

Five dollars! The Indian was speechless. "But Señor," he stammered, "I do not have that much. If you give me a little time, I will look for it."

Roy agreed, since he had to; the Indian disappeared; and that was the last anybody heard of him for months.

Then one morning as Howell and the Judge were sitting on Bean's porch, they heard a creaking and cracking as a ramshackle vehicle came down the trail leading from the main highway. It was a tottering old wagon with boards laid lengthwise on the bed and a pair of moth-eaten burros pulling it. Roy recognized the Indian bridegroom and his still unpaid-for wife behind the burros.

"Sam," he called to his son (Sam was inside the saloon), "bring that man over here." Sam did, and Roy demanded to know where his five dollars was.

"I do not have it, Judge. I do not have as much as that in the world."

"Well," remarked the Judge sternly, "in that case I'll have to divorce you."

The Indian was not sure what that meant and said so. Bean explained in four words:

"No money, no woman."

The Indian had no trouble understanding that. "Give me a little time," he pleaded. "It is possible that I can get the money from my friends."

Roy told him to go ahead, and the couple started off.

"Oh, no you don't!" bellowed Roy. "Leave her here! I'll keep her till you get the money."

Down on the porch sat the patient woman, showing little sign of interest either way. In a short time her man was back with five dollars, happy to think that at last he was married in the sight of God and Roy Bean.

The best people, as well as the Mexican peons, called on Judge Bean to officiate at their weddings. Perhaps his prize job was the double wedding he staged one time for the two daughters of the man who owned the restaurant. Each couple had sent to Del Rio for a license which was due to arrive a sufficient time before the ceremony.

The preliminaries were finished. The guests were assembled. The couples were ready. Then came news that the train was late. Roy put his book away and waited. The couples fretted and fidgeted.

Minutes, then hours slipped by. At last Roy would wait no longer. He lined up his candidates, opened his book, and started in. At the climax of his part of the ceremony he intoned:

"By virtue of the authority vested in me by the State of Texas and the marriage license coming in on Number 10, I now pronounce you man and wife."

The marriages were just as permanent as if Roy had been a bishop. So were several others he handled the same way.

No matter how irregular his proceedings were, Roy found reasons for them which satisfied himself and puzzled his most learned critics. Mostly he used the argument of expediency. When Judge Maxey, another district officer, added his protest to those already registered against granting divorces in a justice court, Roy replied that since the divorcees knew what they wanted and could have taken proper measures by going to Del Rio, the upshot was morally all right. But these people were poor and couldn't have raised money enough to go to Del Rio and pay for correct procedure.

The fact is Roy Bean thought of himself, in the management of his marriage business, not merely as a public convenience, but as a public benefactor.

ORIENTAL INTERLUDE

IT IS TIME NOW to talk about Roy Bean's affair with the Chinaman. The earliest and shortest version of the story appeared in the El Paso *Daily Times* for June 2, 1884.

Here is the latest on Roy Bean:
  Somebody killed a Chinaman and was brought up standing before the irrepressible Roy, who looked through two or three dilapidated law books from stem to stern, and finally turned the culprit loose remarking that he'd be d——d if he could find any law against killing a Chinaman.

That is the core of what has become, after fifty years, one of the best known anecdotes ever to come out of the Southwest. The time must have been about the beginning of 1883 (the ends of track were joined in January). From the west hundreds of Chinese laborers were building. From the east came the Irish and other brawny sons of Europe. The white laborers hated the Chinese for their willingness to work for low wages, their saving ways, their squeaking gibberish, and their love of peace. More killings than one occurred when the gangs from east and west got close enough to rub elbows and cut throats, and there were many narrow escapes. For example take the night in 1882 when the Irish, who had built almost to the east side of the Pecos, got involved in a celebration, and decided their lives would be wasted unless they crossed over to where the Chinese were camped on the west bank and cut off a

few pigtails. They knew that a Chinaman did not like to
fight and would not fight under ordinary provocation, but
would give a satisfactory performance if his pigtail were
cut off. So these drunk and joyful Irishmen organized
themselves and were all ready to start out when the foreman interfered and averted a race riot by a very slim
margin.

Even so, many Chinamen lost their lives by one means
or another and were buried where they fell. Later the
bones of many of them were collected and sent back to the
west coast by Chinese friends who came in for the purpose.

Usually the Americans concerned themselves very little
about whether a Chinaman lived or died, but somehow the
historic case under discussion was brought to Roy Bean
for judgment and he turned the Irishman loose, as most
Americans in West Texas would have been glad of an excuse to do. On account of the feeling between the Chinese
and the other laborers it would have been easy to start
a race riot just then, and Roy knew it. Besides, as he once
said, there were about two hundred of the toughest white
men in the world around the saloon and they might have
lynched him if he hadn't let the Irishman go free. His
decision was merely his own peculiar way of preserving
law and order, at the same time protecting the health of
Judge Bean, but the ruling had the real gamy Western
tang and stuck in men's minds. The story not merely lived;
it grew. By 1899 it was getting into the newspaper ex-
changes this way:

At Langtry, Tex., says the San Francisco Wave, Squire
Roy Bean, who administers justice and keeps the leading
saloon, had to sit in judgment on a railroad clerk who had
killed Ah Ling, a laundry man for, as he claimed, insulting

him. The man was arrested and brought before magistrate Bean, who listened to the evidence, which was given by the accused himself, and then proceeded to turn the pages of the revised statutes: "This here book, which is a Texas law book," he announced, "says that hommyside is th' killin' of a human, male ur female. They is many kinds of hommyside—murder, manslaughter, plain hommyside, negl'gent hommyside, justifi'ble hommyside an' praiseworthy hommyside. They is three kinds of humans—white men, niggers, and Mexicans. It stan's to reason thet if a Chinym'n was human, killin' of him would come under th' head of praiseworthy hommyside. The pris'ner is discharged on condition that he pays f'r havin' th' Chinee buried."

In print and out of print the story went round, gathering details and variations. In the last ten years it has been reprinted a dozen times, and every fresh book about the old days in the Southwest tells it a new way. In 1934, F. H. Bushick put out this version in his book *Glamorous Days:*

Some cavalry soldier in passing through that way, it was thought, had lost his sabre. One of the bridge gang found it. When it was brought into camp nobody wanted the old corn cutter except this Irishman who took a shine to it because he had once been a soldier himself. He ground up the old blade and kept it as a handy weapon, he being a storekeeper of iron supplies, a responsible sort of job.

This Irishman was in the habit of now and then stealing a pie from the cook. The chink got to missing his pies and finally lay for the Irishman and caught him red handed. Armed with a big butcher knife, the chink attacked the Irishman, who ran and got his old sabre and returned to the fray. He made just one pass at the chink with his sabre and cut off his head as clean as if the Lord High Executioner of China had done the job.

A ranger arrested the Irishman and took him before Judge
Bean.

The most remarkable variation of all appeared in 1931
in Tom Rynning's book *Gun Notches*. Tom was an old
cavalryman and peace officer who knew Roy, and this is
the way he tells it:

Once Roy's son shot and killed a Chinaman because he
charged too much for his laundry or something serious like
that, and of course young Bean was tried before his old man.
Naturally Roy wanted to give his boy as easy a deal as the
law would allow, but he was a square-shooter and if his
son turned out guilty of a misdemeanor or anything like that,
it was a cinch he'd wrap it to him just like he was a stranger.

So the Judge opened court with the usual formalities,
throwing out a couple of drunks who wouldn't quit snoring
during the proceedings, and started the justice mill to grind-
ing. On account of his own kin being up for trial, and all the
customers watching him more interested than usual, he went
about things mighty careful and legal-like.

As a rule he give his decisions right out of his deep knowledge of the law, for he'd been a J. P. for a year or more
then; but this time he figured he had to dig into the Un-
abridged Statutes of 1846, or somewheres round that date.

He hooked his spectacles onto his handsome big red nose
and begun reading the law book out loud so's everybody
could see he wasn't keeping any ace in the hole. And damned
if he didn't read those Texas statutes from cover to cover,
cussing every cowpuncher awake that went to sleep on him
and refusing to let any of them go to the bar for a drink
during that long spell of court.

When he'd waded plumb through the Texas law from
murder to cow brands, in about two hours or so, those cow-
punchers and rustlers had got a darned sight more legal

knowledge screwed into their skulls than lots of the tin-horn lawyers of the state ever knew. In fact, they was a plumb nuisance after that, some of them, spouting their information about Texas law by the hour every time they got drunked up and could get some unfortunate dogie to stand hitched long enough to pour it into him by the gallon.

"And there she is, gentlemen," says Roy Bean, when he'd got through. "That's the full unexpurgated law of the great State of Texas up to 1873, and it ain't noways likely there's been any fundamental changes run into since.

"The complete statutes of this here state from the Alamo on ahead, and there ain't a damned line in it nowheres that makes it illegal to kill a Chinaman. The defendant is discharged."

You can ask anybody over forty in West Texas, and many a man under forty, if he knows anything about Roy Bean, and you will get another edition of this same tale. It is already a part of American folk-lore.

The man who shot the Chinaman and started all this storytelling may still be alive. Uncle Bill Jones, who has kept a bar at Reserve, New Mexico, since 1886, says he is, and Uncle Bill was at Langtry when the trial happened. Bill doesn't think he should talk too much about the man, however. "I am not permitted to tell his name," he says. "The last time I heard of him he was tending bar. He is a pleasant sort of person and very agreeable."

Well, people do change!

ROY BEAN—CORONER

JUDGE BEAN's favorite judicial chore was officiating as coroner. Not that he was as fond as all that of dead bodies. He just liked the five dollars he collected every time he served. Stray corpses were always turning up out west of the Pecos and they did much to stabilize Roy's income.

People died for strange reasons in those days. Some got up too early to see well and threw a saddle on somebody else's horse. Others got stray calves tangled up in their loops. Many a man died on account of clerical errors made with a branding iron, and many more passed on because of misplaced confidence in a poker hand or a tendency to dilly-dally in drawing their six-shooters. A very few died of disease or just got tired and lay down for a long rest.

Roy made it legal, no matter how or why they died.

Strangely enough one of the favorite ways of leaving the world in West Texas at that time was falling off a bridge. This was partly because there were so many opportunities and partly because there were so many accidents. The railroad had to build bridges over dozens of arroyos and canyons between San Antonio and El Paso, and most of them were suitable places for a mishap. The high bridge over the Pecos, however, was the most dangerous. It was over three hundred feet above the floor of the canyon and was the natural selection of anyone looking for a bridge to fall off of.

The Pecos high bridge was in Roy's precinct, and in

1892, when it was under construction, he had a coroner's field day running back and forth to view the bodies of its victims. A man named A. J. Reilly fell from a point near the end of the bridge where he was only thirty feet from the ground. He fell on his head, however, and Roy had to ride over and look at him. A stone mason was killed when he got in the way of a falling rock. Three people were drowned in one day by stepping off the pontoon bridge by which the workmen crossed the river—a woman first; then the man who tried to rescue her; then the man who went after Roy Bean to view the bodies. This last death is the only example on record of a person calling the coroner for his own inquest.

Time went on, urged by the ring of picks and the clatter of hammers, and soon the wooden falsework which precedes the steel bridge beams was soaring high above the canyon floor. From below, the workmen looked almost as insignificant as the buzzards circling far overhead. Then one day the top timbers of the structure gave way and plunged ten carpenters down to the rocks three hundred feet beneath.

Seven were killed instantly, says the *Frontier Times*. Three were hurt so badly that there was no possible hope for them. A message was sent to Roy Bean to come and hold another inquest. He came on mule back and found the bodies of the ten men laid out in a row.

He looked at them. He looked at the wreckage of the heavy beams. Then he pronounced over each body, one by one: "This man seems to have come to his death by them big timbers falling on him." The dying men got the same verdict as those already dead.

The coroner's jury, which had been chosen from the onlookers, contained one man who didn't realize that

Judge Bean was always right. He said, "Those three there ain't dead!"

"Say, you gander-eyed galoot," cracked the Judge, "who is running this here inquest? Don't you see them three fellers is bound to die? Do you think I'm damn fool enough to ride thirty miles on a sore-backed mule again to hold another inquest? Officially and legally them fellers is dead, and so I pronounce them dead, every mother's son of 'em, and you will render it as your verdict that they came to their deaths by them big timbers a-fallin' on 'em."

The last of the injured men hung on for three days after he was dead in the sight of the law.

Roy always tried to do (and collect) his bit to settle such cases. The county commissioners allowed him thirty dollars' coroner's fees in a lump in August, 1892, and maybe that was all he got out of the ten carpenters, seven gone and three going.

The story that everybody knows about Roy Bean the coroner comes from another bridge accident which happened a little earlier than this.

It was a Sunday afternoon in February, 1892. A number of bridge carpenters from the Pecos project had come up to pass the day at the Jersey Lily, among them a quiet fellow named Pat O'Brien who didn't care much for the carousing and hell raising that was going on. Towards evening he decided to take a walk. There were no shady lanes or pasture paths in those parts so he started off down the railroad tracks, a smile on his face and a six-shooter in his hip pocket. Why he wanted the weapon is not clear. Maybe he was from the East. Easterners were more careful about this article of dress than native Texans.

When he got to the Myers Canyon bridge, three miles

east of Langtry, a heavy wind was blowing as usual down
the draw, and one gust was strong enough to take him off
his feet and land him at the bottom where the sharp rocks
ended his career. Section workers and track walkers were
always very careful when they crossed this bridge, but the
stranger never suspected his danger until it was too late.

That evening he was found and Roy was notified. He
and Jim King (now of Del Rio) went out in a buckboard,
brought the body back, and laid it out on the table in
the saloon. Nobody knew who the man was beyond his
name, so they searched him for identification and in so
doing found the six-shooter and forty dollars.

"Now," said Coroner Bean, "I've got to bury this poor
devil and it's hard digging in these rocks. I hereby fine this
defendant forty dollars for carrying concealed weapons."

Turning to Jim King he added, "Don't you think that's
the way to handle it, Jimmy?" Jimmy thought so, and Roy
had no idea that he had made a historic decision, but one
man told another and pretty soon Texas was chuckling
again at Roy Bean's way of conducting his business. The
San Antonio *Express* got hold of the story of Roy's verdict
in March and passed it on to the world.

"Gentlemen," said Roy to the jury and onlookers,
"there is nothing to find out how that man came to his
death. He fell from the bridge and that's all there is about
it. But there is one thing that is not so plain, and that is
what was he doing with that gun? Of course he is dead
and can't explain, but that ain't the fault of the law; it's
his own misfortune. Justice is justice, and law is law,
and as he can't offer no satisfactory explanation of the
matter I shall be obliged to fine him forty dollars for carrying on or about his person that pistol. Because a man
chooses to put on a pair of wings is no reason why the

great State of Texas should not have what is coming to her all the same."

A few hours after the inquest the body was buried. It was not buried very deep in the stony soil, and the coffin was a plain wooden box, but some of that forty dollars was needed to do what was done.

At least one other time, Roy fined a dead body. It was about a year later when two Mexicans got into a squabble at Painted Cave. One was shot in the mouth and killed. Roy found a pistol on him and ten dollars, which he kept. Maybe he was just seeing if the same system would work twice.

One last episode in Roy's career as coroner brings in some family history. In the 1890's, before his troubles came upon him, Roy was fairly well-to-do. He had at one time five herds of sheep, and a herd at full strength was composed of about three thousand head. There was a *pastor* with each herd, and a *vicario* who made the rounds taking supplies to the *pastores* and checking up on things.

Roy left most of this business to his son Sam, but when a *pastor* got too insistent about the yearly settlement, or when thieves were active, Roy sometimes took at least a verbal part. M. W. Tracy once heard him say to Sam, "If you see a Greaser within five miles of that flock of sheep, pull on them. If you miss, you may ask them what in hell they are doing there."

Apparently Sam didn't always miss. One day a man came in to report to the Judge that a dead man's bones had been found in a canyon west of Langtry in the bend of the river. Roy listened to the report, then told Sam, who was standing by, to go out after the remains. Sam's horse was ready saddled, as usual, outside the saloon. He picked up a gunny sack and started off.

"But you don't know where it is," put in the man who had found the body.

"I know where it is," said Sam.

Some hours later he came back with a bag full of bones which he laid at one side of the porch.

At this time J. P. Torres was the legally constituted justice of the peace, and hearing of an inquest to be held he could see no reason why he shouldn't be the man to hold it. Therefore he looked the land over, noted the position of the bag of bones on Roy's porch, and sent a Mexican around behind to see if he could steal it.

The Mexican crept around behind the saloon unobserved, got his hands on the bag, and started to twitch it slowly around the corner. Roy happened to step outside at the moment and the look of surprise on his face when he saw those bones move was something to remember. He jumped a mile. By the time he was thinking normally again the Mexican was gone—without the bones.

Roy held his inquest right away. He held it after a hasty peep into the sack which revealed a bullet hole in the forehead of a mouldering skull.

"I rule," he said in his best official manner, "that this hombre met his death by being shot by a person unknown who was a damn good shot."

There was a sequel to this story which W. H. Dodd, the storekeeper, used to tell. Roy asked his friend to get out a grocery box for a coffin and bury the remains. Dodd was willing to oblige and when the bones were stowed away and the lid nailed down, he called the Judge to see if the job suited him. Roy took one look and hit the roof. He saw his own name on the box, for the groceries originally shipped in it had been sent to him.

"Hell," he boomed, "you can't bury him in that box!

Why, it's got my name right on the top. What if somebody dug him up some day and thought it was me?"

So Mr. Dodd took off the lid, turned the boards over,
and nailed them down again. Then the box was regularly
planted.

Only once did Roy get in dutch over his rulings as
coroner. This was in connection with the fining of the
corpse of the man who blew off the Myers Canyon bridge.
The county officials at Del Rio decided to investigate him
and called him in. Roy pleaded that he needed the con-
fiscated money to bury the corpse. "You wouldn't want
the poor fellow to go without a Christian burial, would
you?" he demanded.

The officials thought they wouldn't and Roy got off.

JUDGE BEAN FINDS HIMSELF FAMOUS AND SPENDS HIS LAST
TWENTY YEARS TRYING TO LIVE UP TO HIS REPUTATION.

"Them ain't grapes," said Oscar to the traveling salesman. "Them's eyeballs. We had a fight here last night."

The Judge was a kind-hearted, good old man who debauched himself with drink and who, as Dan Jackson used to say, could fly higher and light lower than most any man in the country.

W. D. Greet of El Paso.

HOT SPOT

IT WAS BARELY DAYLIGHT when the train stopped at Langtry to take on water. Nobody was up. Not a chimney was smoking. The only sound audible was the steaming and singing of the engine talking to itself by the water tank.

Fifteen minutes to wait! The traveling salesman in the end seat of the smoking car uncoiled himself, brushed the soot off his lapels, and stepped off the train for a breath of air. There was the Jersey Lily ten steps away, the front door open. Like everybody else who came to Langtry the salesman pointed himself automatically for that open door.

Nobody was inside but Oscar Sweden, Roy Bean's roustabout, who was busy sweeping up. After an exchange of good mornings the salesman looked around for something to talk about.

"My!" he said, "you raise nice grapes here."

"Grapes? We don't raise no grapes here. Where do you see any grapes?"

"There on the floor."

"Hell, Mister, them ain't grapes. Them's eyeballs. We had a fight here last night."

This was the kind of story people used to pass around when Langtry was in flower. In spite of Roy Bean's boast that he had brought law to the Pecos country, his town was notorious as one of the hottest spots on the border —a center for all sorts of sin and corruption.

Naturally there were many fine people living there, the kind who make up the backbone of every Western town. You could trust them with your last dollar or your dying wish. They would stay with you if you got in trouble. They could fight and smile and live hard and treat a stranger like one of themselves. Oh yes, there were plenty of people like that, but there were also others, and it was these others who gave the place its bad name: men with blood on their hands, crooked ranchers, cattle rustlers, smugglers, gunmen, gamblers, and assorted desperadoes of all kinds. Many of them were there because it was only a few yards to Mexico. The rest just happened in.

To keep this mob from reverting to a state of nature was often too much for the local peace officers. Detachments of troops were stationed near Langtry once or twice, and the Texas Rangers were always dropping in to see about something that needed correction.

The ones who came to grief were, as a rule, the ones who were looking for trouble, and it was not every day, or even every week, that they found what they were looking for. The bad times came when the toughs got together for an evening of social pleasure in one of the saloons. Those were the occasions when sober citizens had to hunt for cover.

Mrs. Simon Shaw came out to the Pecos in '83 and spent part of her girlhood in a small house on the hill just behind the Jersey Lily. Many a time she pulled a mattress off the bed and slept on the dining-room floor for fear of stray bullets. Twenty-three men were killed in her neighborhood, she says, in two years.

Hell on Wheels faded into the past. Sheriffs and justice courts became common as dirt. Kerosene lamps, parlor organs, safety bicycles, and other refinements came to

Langtry, but it continued to be a hot spot. Christmas, 1888, was a typically wild time. Soldiers, railroad men, and cowboys got together for a grand free-for-all. Roy Bean's saloon was a focal point for the great carouse and somebody didn't like the way he handled his responsibilities. In the middle of the night this somebody took a pot shot at the Judge's front door, aiming at the corner of the room where he usually slept. The shot ranged high and did severe execution on a shelf of canned fruit, cove oysters, and other delicacies just over the bed. Roy was not damaged except for a few bruises caused by his carelessness in failing to open the screen door when he came steaming into the open, gun in hand. In a few days all the Texas papers had the story.

About this same time the Reverend Winter Green came out from Del Rio to take charge of the first religious service ever held in Langtry.

Mr. Green was doing a little missionary work for the Baptist Church and thought he ought to put in some time where he was really needed. They told him to go see what Roy Bean thought about it.

"Well, Preacher," said Roy roughly, giving the young man a sidewise swipe with his hard eye, "I'll let you go ahead if you really want to preach and ain't come out here to nose into other folks' business."

He meant he didn't want the beer market interfered with.

"Where can I find a suitable building?" inquired Mr. Green.

"Take that empty salt house over there and I'll see you ain't disturbed."

So the Reverend Winter Green preached to a small congregation. He led the hymns and took the collection

and started on the benediction. Just then hell broke loose
outside. The boom of forty-fives filled the little building
and drowned out the preacher's voice.

Mr. Green was always proud of that congregation.
They actually waited until he finished the benediction
before they rushed out to see what all the shooting was for.

When he got to the door himself he saw that there had
been a gunfight. The loser's body had fallen almost across
the threshold.

In addition to the regular sprees and shootings which
kept the town livened up, there were bitter disagreements
among the local cattlemen. Rustling and smuggling of
livestock went on under cover all the time. Roy himself
was arrested by the rangers on August 21, 1891, for
smuggling horses, and turned loose after a hearing in San
Antonio. In 1893 the two factions which were quarreling
about running stolen cattle across the river became so
irritated with each other that the rangers had great difficulty in averting a cattleman's war. After that things
gradually quieted down, but every once in a while something would happen to remind people that this was still
the Wild West.

The late W. D. Greet of El Paso, who once lived at
Langtry, saw plenty of excitement as late as 1902. He
used to tell of the time a man named Watts shot a one-
eyed Mexican sheepherder named Emeterio. "I remember
when Watts killed Emeterio," said Mr. Greet one time.
"Emeterio fell in front of my house. I was on a scout
with the rangers and was gone three or four days. The
Judge did not want to let them move Emeterio out of the
road, because he attracted people and made business good.
My wife and my boy, who was about four or five months
old, were alone in the house except for the cook and

another servant, so Dodd took them up to his house and kept them until I got back. In the meanwhile the ants hollowed out old Emeterio so there wasn't anything left of him except his overalls, his jumper, and his hide. They completely destroyed all of him that was inside of his skin. I shall never forget those ants—we used to catch them and put them in a saucer and make them fight."

Signs of civilization kept on appearing. A one-room schoolhouse opened for business in the middle eighties. Church services became more frequent as the years went by. The young people had fun with picnics in Pump Canyon and parties at their homes. Still Langtry was a hot spot for many years, and eyeballs on the floor of the Jersey Lily were well within the bounds of possibility.

JUDGE BEAN AT HOME

On Roy Bean's special page in the great gallery of Western portraits is the picture which posterity seems to want to remember. It isn't such a pretty picture, but it has character. There stands your primitive American, a tough old man, solid on his feet, arrogant, suspicious, and sardonic, with a look in his eye which says, "I'm Judge Bean. Who the hell might you be?"

This would be Roy Bean between 1885 and 1895 when he was on top of the world, or anyway the portion of it along the Pecos River. On the surface he didn't look much like the California dandy of thirty-five years before. Except for special occasions he didn't bother much about cleaning up. His corpulent stomach flopped down over his belt. His shirt tail often blossomed out in the back and large areas of underwear showed through the gaps in front. When he wore a vest he buttoned only the top button. The bandanna around his neck and the Mexican sombrero which he adopted in his last years added a characteristic note to his get-up, but not the old touch of gaudy frontier elegance.

There were times, however, when he spruced up, especially when some of the mighty men of the land wanted to meet him. The railroad officials, who had better opportunities than most to know of his exploits, sometimes wired him to get on a special car or train at Langtry. He would rustle up a basin of water and hold his head over it while his daughters washed the debris out of his thick, grizzled beard. Then he would put on his Prince Albert coat and plug hat (yes, he had them!) and strut out to board the special. He would ride to San Antonio or El Paso enjoying his hosts' liquor and cigars while his hosts enjoyed him. There was a special flavor about his personality. You knew before he said "By God——" in his heavy voice that he was a character right out of covered-wagon days.

Other things besides his appearance had changed since '49. He was more cautious now about getting into arguments with dangerous men, though his explosive temper was still on tap and when he got good and mad he could make most people step lively. Sometimes he went after his gun, particularly if the other fellow didn't look too pugnacious, but he never hurt anybody. Much of his wrath he took out in high-powered bursts of profanity. He could cuss in two languages by the hour and was not guilty of too much repetition, either.

In fairness it should be said that in the presence of women his Southern breeding rose up and made him a little more careful of his language and deportment.

Financially he was doing all right. Beginning with the one-room dive on the south side of the railroad in 1883, he increased his business until he was able to move into the big saloon across the tracks. Somebody burned this one down for him in 1898 and he replaced it with the little building now standing at Langtry. Most people suppose that this last is the original Jersey Lily, and all but a few old-timers have forgotten what a big place Roy ran before the fire and other troubles cleaned him out.

The old saloon was a long building with a hall down the middle and an L at the back. At the front were two rooms in which he did his buying and selling. Behind these were dining and sleeping rooms, and in the angle of the L was a corral and wagon yard with sleeping quarters for cowboys and teamsters opening off it.

Special accommodations were provided for the four-footed boarders which Roy always entertained. Facing the railroad along the front of his property was a row of cages for the bears, wildcats, panthers, coyotes, and other animals in his menagerie. He kept a number of them around all the time, partly because they were good for business and partly because he enjoyed their company.

In the two rooms at the front of his building Roy carried on his business. To the left of the entrance was his store and to the right was his holy of holies, the bar-and-court room. This last was about fifteen by thirty feet with the bar running crosswise of the east side. The pool table (on which Roy's son Sam often slept) stood in the middle of the floor. Beyond it in the rear corner Roy had a musty goat's nest of a shakedown where he did his own sleeping. The other corner was occupied by a whiskey barrel and odds and ends of harness, horse feed, blankets, ropes, tools and what not.

This room was usually filthy and it cost Roy a supreme effort to clean it up. Straw packing from the barrels of bottled beer strewed the floor, punctuated here and there by all the nameless objects which gather in public rooms. Once Ranger Ed Aten and some of his fellow officers got disgusted looking at so much filth and threatened to do their drinking at Torres' bar across the tracks if Roy didn't clean up. So he got in a couple of Mexicans and gave the place the going over it had needed for years. When he rebuilt after the fire he put an iron grating in front of the bar so some kinds of foreign matter would drop on through and save cleaning.

The rebuilt Jersey Lily was much smaller than the old saloon. It had only one room, no living quarters in the rear, and no wagon yard. A lean-to for a new pool table was added but no further expansion was ever called for.

In the days of his glory in the big saloon Roy had his family with him. He brought his children out from San Antonio as soon as he had a place for them and immediately went to work bringing them up. There were five of them. John, the oldest, Roy said he had "adopted," but the other four—Roy, Laura, Zulema, and Sam—he claimed proudly as his own. There are various theories as to how John and the rest of the children were related.

Roy thought a good deal of his boys and girls. In fact he was fond of all children and left many pleasant memories among the Langtry youngsters who used to listen to his stories and ride his old dun horse Bayo.

His own family did not stay intact very long. Children left home early in those days, and one by one the younger Beans began to find places of their own. John left after a very brief stay with his foster father, became a ranch hand, and was a familiar figure on the sheep ranches around Dryden until his death in the early 1940's. Little Roy said goodbye next and went to work for the railroad. Zulema and Sam, the two youngest, went to school for a while. Then the girls married, leaving only Sam at home. He was around until the Judge died, sometimes damning his father's old-fashioned notions but getting on with him fairly well. Roy thought the world of Sam—always trusted him and never complained of his wild ways.

The girls were the ones who kept their old man awake nights. Bringing up two attractive young ladies in the Jersey Lily was a risky business and it is to Roy's credit that he did a good job. Everybody agrees that the daughters developed into fine young women, but their father had some bad moments over them.

Their room was directly behind the saloon with only a flimsy partition between, and they lived there in the worst times without much company except an old parlor organ on which they learned to play a little. When the crowd in front got noisy and obscene, Roy used to put his head through the door of the girls' room and holler, "Come on girls, play something, will you?" They would grind out a few tunes on the organ, and their father always felt that by this means he had kept bad language out of the boudoir.

The only time he was not good to his girls was when he had been drinking, or when they were careless about their daughterly responsibilities.

They used to pay daily visits to Mrs. Simon Shaw in those days. Mrs. Shaw was recently married and had moved into a near-by house. One day Roy came up to her place carrying his sawed-off shotgun and looking for his daughters. The shotgun was his symbol of authority. He always carried it when he went after somebody, though he seldom loaded it and didn't even own a cartridge to fit it when he died.

The girls saw him coming and begged Mrs. Shaw to hide them, so she put them behind the headboard of a high old wooden bed. "You keep quiet," she said. "Don't move."

Roy stomped up to the door and demanded information about his young 'uns. "I ought to kill 'em!" he bellowed.

"My goodness, what have they done?" asked Mrs. Shaw, peeping cautiously out.

"They don't cook for me."

"Haven't you had any breakfast?"

"No."

"Well, come in and I'll get you some."

After breakfast he felt better and Mrs. Shaw said, "Now you go on home and don't you talk that way any more."

"All right," said Roy, "I won't," and he stomped off.

Later in the day a boy came to the house and told Mrs. Shaw that the Judge wanted the girls to come down and cook his supper.

"Oh, we don't dare go alone!" shivered Laura. "Come with us, Mrs. Shaw."

So Mrs. Shaw went along and helped, but she left a lecture behind her. "You don't have anything to do but clean up that little room," she told the girls. "You get up mornings and cook breakfast."

After that there was no more trouble.

The girls did well when it came time to pick out husbands. Laura married a construction foreman named Billy Mellor who studied engineering and rose in his profession. Zulema became the wife of a prosperous citizen named Henry Voss. Roy always referred proudly to Mellor and Voss as his sons, and they were kind and respectful to him. The daughters, both widows and the only ones left of Roy Bean's children, now live in New Orleans at adjoining addresses keeping a determined silence about themselves and their father.

To get back to the Jersey Lily, it must be admitted that although Roy kept an eye on his daughters in the back room he preferred the barroom to the bower. He drank his own beer and played pool on his own table when business was slack. Incidentally he was a first-class pool player. Ranger Aten used to play with him whenever he came to Langtry, and always lost. Roy would console him by saying, "Well, it's worth fifty cents to say you played pool with the Law West of the Pecos."

When even pool and beer were beginning to grow monotonous, Roy would sit on the gallery in his rocking chair and talk things over with anybody who wanted to loaf with him. He did lots of rocking-chair sitting.

At train time there was a flurry of business. The west-bound train, due at six P.M., stopped half an hour while the passengers got dinner in the station eating house. Other trains halted fifteen or twenty minutes. Both short and long stops were good enough for a visit to the Jersey Lily, and for those who didn't care to pay his place a call Roy provided a convenience in the shape of a two-wheeled cart on which he carried bottled beer to the train.

Most of his visitors were attracted as much by Bean as by beer. The signs plastered across his saloon: JUDGE ROY BEAN NOTARY PUBLIC. LAW WEST OF THE PECOS. THE JERSEY LILLY—were bait enough, but by now Roy himself was notorious and a great tourist attraction. Every train brought old and new acquaintances, and even ladies took their virtue in their hands to set foot inside his tavern. Nothing pleased the old man so much as public attention, and he displayed himself conscientiously on his porch at train time so people would see him.

His visitors found him an interesting talker with a dry, quick humor which usually flashed out unexpectedly. He was always coming back at somebody as he did at the stranger who panted in for a bottle of beer on a hot day. The man took a swallow and then said in disgust, "I thought you advertised iced beer."

"Why, hell!" said Roy, "whoever heard of ice in July in Texas?"

Everybody stopped at the Jersey Lily, but the callers who got the best reception were the ones who needed it most. No hungry man was refused a handout at the back door. Consequently every tramp in the country made it a point to turn up with a sad and plausible story whenever he was in Roy's neighborhood.

Sometimes one of these transients would try to take the old man in, and then there was trouble. Ambrose Burdwell, who was an observing little boy then, saw him handle one case.

It began when a pitiful specimen came hobbling in with one leg in heavy bandages leaning on a green stick.

"Oh, my poor leg!" he groaned. "I got to get to a doctor quick. Where can I find one?"

"There ain't no doctor this side of Del Rio," said Roy.

"My God, I can't walk and I've got no money! Oh, what shall I do?"

Roy thought for a minute and then took off his hat. "Fork over, boys," he said. "We've got to buy this hombre a ticket."

A few dollars dropped into the hat. The man accepted the money with thanks and went out, his pain much relieved. His condition was, in fact, so much improved that Roy became suspicious and sent a boy out after him. The boy came back and reported that the tramp was with two companions in a shed up the track bragging about taking the country boys in.

Roy had him yanked back to the Jersey Lily.

"Now," he said, "let me see that leg. I'm a kind of a doctor myself."

The bystanders wrestled off shoe and sock, cut off one leg of the man's pants, and found him sound as a nut. Roy shook his head, however. "That leg's got to come off," he said. "Dr. José (José was a half-witted Mexican roustabout), bring me my *zeruche*."

When José brought an old rusty saw, the tramp began

to throw his weight around, but the boys carried him inside and held him down on a table.

"We better make the cut about here," said Roy, giving the leg a good rasp with the saw.

"No, you're too high. You want to leave as much stump as you can," objected one of the others, seizing the saw and gouging several square inches of hide off the tramp's shin.

"You're both wrong!" yelled a third, and barked the leg again.

As the quarrel grew louder and louder the rumble of an approaching freight train tickled the tramp's ears. In the midst of the uproar he saw his chance, exploded through the door minus shoe, sock, and half his pants, and went up the side of a box car like a squirrel. He was never seen in Langtry again.

Not many put anything over on Roy, but he was full of Scotch tricks himself. They say he had a lump of glass on the back bar which he used to drop into a cocktail so it would make a tinkling sound like ice when he stirred it around. After the tinkle he would fish it out and lay it on the back bar again. Everett Lloyd declares in his little book on Roy Bean that he used to set a lighted candle in the stove in the winter time, figuring that the glimmer of light would fool people into thinking they were warm.

Another of his tricks was to be taken with a severe back-ache when he got a little ahead in a poker game. He and his winnings would drop out with dreadful groans. It became proverbial around Langtry to say, when somebody was trying to get out of something, "There goes your goddam back again!"

Once Roy and Old Man Babb were having a poker game in the Jersey Lily. Babb stepped outside, leaving his gun on the chair. Roy took out the cartridges and when Babb came back accused him of cheating. They nearly had a very interesting fight.

Another time the proprietor of the restaurant, which in the very early days was set up near the station in an old passenger coach, fell out with the Judge. Roy swore the man owed him money and the man swore he had paid the debt. Roy waited until the eating house was having a rush of business one day. Then he buckled on his gun belt, went over and stood in the door while the customers were leaving, and diverted the meal money from the cash drawer into his own pocket.

Even the Mexicans suffered from his more or less benevolent despotism. When a sheepherder came into the saloon Roy usually greeted him with "¡*Tu me debes!* ¡*Págame!*" "You owe me money! Pay me!" If the Mexican couldn't be persuaded that he was in Roy's debt, there were other ways of getting at him. Once Roy offered to sell a sheepherder a fine six-shooter for ten dollars. The gun and the price were both good and the sheepherder bit hard.

"Now," said Roy, "it's against the law to carry this, so I'll wrap it up for you." He reached down behind the bar for a piece of paper, and when he came up a cheap Smith and Wesson five-shooter was in the paper which the Mexican carried away.

Tactics like these do not make a man the idol of old and young in his home town, and Roy had some earnest enemies. When he wanted a man to like him, however, he was generally able to put himself over. It made no difference who was to be impressed; Roy's nerve was equal to the occasion.

One man he had always wanted to meet was Jay Gould, and when he heard in 1890 that Mr. Gould was coming through on a special train, he made up his mind to do something about it. First he got in some special champagne, according to J. C. Tolman who tells the story in the *Texaco Star*. Then he cleaned up his place and himself and strolled down to the station. When the Gould special came rattling into Langtry he calmly took the red bandanna from around his neck and waved it at the engineer. Thinking that a bridge must be out at the very least, the engineer put on his brakes and brought the special to a screeching stop.

Mr. Gould poked his head out of a window to see what was happening and immediately found himself in conversation with Roy Bean. Before he knew it he, his daughter, his doctor, and the station agent were sitting in the Jersey Lily sipping Roy's champagne and eating the ladyfingers for which Mr. Gould sent back to his private car. When the party broke up—regretfully—the agent went back to his post to find the wires buzzing. He hastened to answer his call, and this, says Mr. Tolman, was the message he received:

Where hell you been? What hell matter? Gould special passed you three hour. Should been Del Rio two hours ago. Hasn't reached Comstock. Been calling. Why hell don't you stay on job? Must be ditched. May fell off High Bridge. For God's sake get section crew and find out. Reported New York Gould killed in wreck. Stock Exchange wild. Trains piled up all over division. Answer quick.

To which the agent replied:

Jay G. been visiting Judge Roy Bean and me. Been eating ladyfingers and champagne. Take your old job and go to hell. Special just lett.

When all other forms of amusement failed at the Jersey Lily it was always possible to hold court. As Roy got older and Langtry grew calmer, these occasions lost a good deal of their old-time spirit. In fact, after 1890 or thereabouts Roy used his judicial powers mostly to stimulate business. The trials were conducted with a burlesque overtone and the men who hung around the saloon didn't take them as anything more than a good excuse for a drunk. The prisoner, however, sometimes failed to detect the comedy, particularly if he was new in those parts.

That brings up the only trial in which Roy sentenced a prisoner to be hanged.

It was some time in the late nineties. A man named Murphy was the roadmaster at the time, and one day he telegraphed from Pumpville a few miles up the line that his wallet and six-shooter had been taken from a traveling bag which he had left in the caboose of a freight train. Would the boys at Langtry look out for three young men coming down the track?

Before long the three thieves were seen up the line. One of them was burying something which was later found to be Mr. Murphy's six-shooter. They took the boys into custody, found the money, and discussed what to do next. Two of the youngsters seemed humble enough about their crime, so they were turned loose with a bucket of water—it being a long way to the next drink. The third thief, however, was a tall, one-eyed young desperado who cut at Sam Bean with a knife and cussed and swore a blue streak.

"You can shut up," said Roy coldly. "We're going to *hang* you."

Painstakingly they arranged the courtroom while the boy got paler and more nervous.

"Now Billy," said Roy to storekeeper Dodd after various people had been designated as attorneys, bailiffs, and clerks, "now Billy, you act as clergyman and help this rascal pray for his soul, because by God he's going to need it."

The boy's knees gave way and he decided to pray right there. He and Billy Dodd knelt down on the porch of the Jersey Lily, and how they did lay themselves out in prayer! When they were prayed out, the trial began, but two or three times during the proceedings Billy Dodd and the boy stopped for a little more spiritual refreshment. When this happened the judge and jury seized the opportunity to take some refreshment of another kind.

After the evidence was all in and the jury had pronounced the prisoner guilty, Roy delivered the sentence in his best rafter-rattling courtroom voice:

"—to be hanged by the neck till you are dead, and the Lord have mercy on your soul!"

"Oh, Judge," wailed the hysterical youngster. "Shoot me if you have to, but don't hang me!"

"No," replied Roy. "The law says you got to hang."

"Then for God's sake let me write a letter to my mother."

"Go ahead," agreed the Judge. So the boy wrote a heartbreaker which everybody read over his shoulder, and then they took him out to hang him.

There being no trees to use as a gallows, a cowboy threw his rope across a box car. The noose was dropped over the condemned boy's head, and Billy Dodd's prayers rose in a grand finale. Just then the cowboy who owned the rope figured it was time to wind up the business and he started off at a gallop. The rope almost tightened, and if it had, the young criminal would have had his head jerked off. The cowboy's horse fortunately ran into another one just at that moment and Billy Dodd had time to slip the noose over the boy's head.

"Run like hell!" he said, and the boy ran. Such running had never been seen in Langtry before, but at that moment a couple of the boys posted up the draw fired off their six-shooters, and then the runner bettered his own record.

"There wasn't any use sending him to Del Rio to be tried," says Mrs. Dodd, reminiscently. "He would have rotted in jail for no telling how long since he had no money to pay a fine. It was better to let him go. Judge Bean said that the fright was good for him and he'd probably never do wrong again."

The sequel to this story says that several years later a tall, one-eyed young man dropped in at the Jersey Lily and said to Roy, "You don't remember me, do you?"

"Can't say I do," said Roy.

"Well, I'm the fellow you almost hanged a few years back. You know I told a friend of yours about that trial and he said I should have known it was just a joke. Well, that got me to thinking and I decided to brace up and go back to my mother. I sure thank you for teaching me a lesson."

No, the Law West of the Pecos was not doing much serious work in the courtroom during the last ten years of his life, but he was always good for a hilarious hour or two seasoned with equal parts of beer and law. When he stepped out on his porch and hollered, "Court, boys!" everybody within hearing galloped over with a happy grin on his face. If it was an evening trial the celebration never broke up until late. And every trial was nicely timed so that beer and legal proceedings were finished about the same time.

ROY BEAN MINDS HIS OWN BUSINESS

"ONE PINT. That'll be thirty-five cents. You want what? Change? We don't give change out here; you get back on the train. I said you better get back on the train or it'll go off and leave you. Yes, you gave me a twenty-dollar gold piece and I'm telling you that any galoot from New York with no more sense than to pay for a beer with a twenty-dollar gold piece ain't got any change coming.

"Oh, I'm a bastard am I? Well now listen, young man, I'm the Law West of the Pecos and I hereby declare that court's in session. I fine you nineteen dollars and sixty-five cents for disturbing the peace. If you open your trap I'll double the fine and hold you here till it's paid.

"There! I guess that'll learn him not to get gay with an old man. Look at him get on that train."

Little scenes like that were common at the Jersey Lily. Roy Bean dearly loved a dollar and froze onto every coin that came within reach of his sticky fingers. The no-change racket was just one of his tricks but it was the one which got him the most publicity. Everybody except the victim thought it was very funny. All the spectators laughed heartily, peddled the story around, and thus caused others to come in and be cheated.

The more Roy got himself talked about, the more money he made. Not since those first years in San Antonio had he given off such an odor of prosperity. Before very long he was cultivating half a dozen side lines and trying to make two dollars grow where two bits had grown before. One of these side lines was sheep raising. As little affinity as there was between Roy Bean and a sheep, he liked to think of himself as a sheepman and at one time had three large herds browsing and baa-ing out on the hills. Along with the sheep he encouraged a few goats to grow up so he could butcher them and sell the meat. There was also a bunch of hogs which rooted around his gallery and had adventures under the trains which paused out in front. All of Roy's livestock made money for him except the pigs. It took a good deal of faith, hope and trickery to make them pay off.

The Judge was worrying about them one day when a hungry tramp shuffled in, got a handout, and sat down to relax. "Sam," Roy said to his son just at that moment, "you write a letter to San Antonio for some more corn for them hogs."

"How much do you pay for feed now?" piped up the tramp.

Roy told him, and the tramp did some rapid mental arithmetic. "Why man, do you realize," said he at last, "that those hogs are costing you twenty-five cents a pound? You can buy them on the hoof in Dallas for ten or fifteen."

Roy looked thoughtful for a while but finally his face cleared up. "You go on and write that letter," he said to Sam. "If I do any more figuring I'm liable not to have any hogs left."

He had other close shaves with his pigs. One of them occurred when he took somebody else in as a partner in the pork-raising business. He soon found out—but Roy's brother Sam wrote the story down one time and we'll let him tell it:

Judge Roy Bean Again

A man came to Roy once and says to him, Judge I have found a good place for a Hog Ranch down the River here and I want to go into the business. I think it will be a paying enterprise and as you have more money than I have you can advance the necessary funds to set the scheme on foot. Very well says Roy I am always willing to go into anything that there is any money in. Enough said, the Hog Ranch was established, and it flourished for about two years, but Roy was not receiving any profits from the Ranch hitherto it had all been unlimited expenditure without results and Roy proposed to his partner to have a dissilution of partnership. But he objected and the Ranch had to wag along in the same old way. Roy wanted to bring suit against him, but there was no other court or authority except his own and what was he to do. Finally after a deep study an Idea struck him and he says now I have it, I will sue him before myself. He issued a citation for his partner who made his appearance in court. Roy made a speech in his own behalf and testified in the case while his partner viewed the proceedings with silent amazement and had but little to say. The decision of the court in this case is briefly this the Plaintiff who is the court itself will take one half the Hogs and the other half the constable will sell at public auction to pay the damages suffered by this Plaintiff and the cost of suit.

Samuel G. Bean
Las Cruces

To supplement his wealth on the hoof, Roy had a gold mine. It was not a hole in the ground requiring pick, shovel, and sweat. Roy wouldn't have been interested in that. Pen, ink, and a good imagination were the tools he usually used, and with them he got out some pretty rich ore from time to time.

Not to be too mysterious about it, Roy Bean's gold mine was the Southern Pacific System.

From the first the railroad company did all it could for Judge Bean, probably on account of his good service in cleaning up the construction camps in '82. Several times the officials took active steps to help him get ahead, but he was not willing to let it go at that. Whenever he got a chance to gouge a little extra out of the System, he did so. Perhaps the men in charge realized that he was the kind of person who would rather pick up what he wanted by using his wits than take it as a gift. Anyway they let him get away with modified murder every now and then. One time an old burro from the Bean stables decided he would not move off the track even if a train was coming. When they had swept him off the right of way Roy wrote a letter. He asked the Southern Pacific to soothe his grief for the loss of his "prize Kentucky jack" and estimated that fifteen hundred dollars would be enough to make him feel better.

The General Manager's office detected a faint odor of fish in this demand and decided to ask a few questions. They wrote to H. L. Howell, an employee stationed near Langtry. "What was that mule really worth?" they asked.

"In my judgment," Mr. Howell wrote back, "the animal was worth about fifty cents."

"Why?" demanded the higher-ups by return mail.

"Because he was old and blind and couldn't even find his own way around," replied Howell. And to himself he added that if Roy was doing business as usual he had probably taken the old burro out and tied him to the tracks.

With Howell's report and their own experience to enlighten them, the officials must have known what was what. Nevertheless they chose to settle with Roy Bean for five hundred dollars.

And they continued to contribute in various and sundry ways. One was by having train wrecks. Freight trains traveled faster than they do now and had trouble oftener, which was all right with the natives. One train loaded with dry goods kept Langtry in hats and shoes for months. Another famous crash upset a cargo of California wine at the horseshoe curve between Pumpville and Langtry. Immediately every hobo between El Paso and San Antonio galloped up and prostrated himself beside the ruby rill that trickled for two days from the wreck. A pool formed down the canyon and some of the bums took off their shoes and stepped in so as to be able to brag later of wading in a lake of pure wine.

Then in the early 90's there was a wreck which Roy made all his own. A heavy train came to grief trying to cross a canyon on a bridge that wasn't there. Several car-loads of unrefined beet sugar were tipped off the track with the rest of the freight. The section crews were called out at once to clear the track of wreckage and Roy Bean, Jr., was sent out with lantern and pistol to act as night watchman. This played right into the hands of Roy, Sr. Nightly he sent out mules and wagons and took away many loads of sugar which he stored somewhere and sold to his Mexican customers for several years after. He figured, with much logic, that somebody might as well get a little good out of that sugar and no doubt he felt justified when a flash flood came down the canyon shortly after the wreck and washed away what was left.

For years the scene of the smash-up was known as Sugar Canyon in memory of Roy's attempt at cornering the sugar market.

The railroad company knew about his operations but never asked for an accounting.

And so the years went on while Judge Bean kept his half-dozen irons in the fire, but all the time he was hammering away at his real job which was keeping a saloon. Forty years before he had learned the business from his brothers in Chihuahua and California, and ever since he had been happiest when he had a bar and a bottle on hand. Having done so much of his beer vending under pioneer conditions, he did not go in for crystal mirrors and mahogany fittings. A tent saloon, simple and movable, just about suited him, and when he invested in something a little more permanent his place kept some of the rough-and-ready atmosphere of the boom-town gin mill. The Jersey Lily was long on saturation and short on swank. Roy liked it that way.

By one method or another he cornered most of the town's liquor business, but he had opposition. J. P. Torres kept a place called the Eagle's Nest on the south side of the tracks, and for a time a tent saloon known as the Blue Goose was operated by the Radliff brothers across the draw just east of the Jersey Lily. The proprietors of the Blue Goose and the Eagle's Nest used to call Roy's place the Buzzard's Roost.

Torres was the only rival who gave Roy any trouble and that didn't happen very often. Occasionally, however, the sparks flew. A tale used to be told by Mr. J. W. Schofield of San Antonio about the time a sheep raiser of the region was preparing to pay off about three hundred sheep shearers. That meant money for somebody and Roy didn't see why he should be left out in the cold. He proceeded at once to get an extra stock of beer and whiskey. Torres heard what was going on and decided he would make a grab too. He had at the time (it was the spring of 1893) a partner running a dance hall and saloon at Flanders, a construction camp a few miles east of the Pecos high bridge which was then being completed. Torres got word to his partner to send the dance-hall girls to Langtry to help the sheep shearers celebrate. With great secrecy the transfer of the girls and a Mexican orchestra was accomplished.

"Soon after the arrival of the dancers," the tale continues, "strains of music issued from Torres' place to the accompaniment of shifting feet. The crowd of Mexicans in Judge Bean's saloon, one by one, raised their lips from the glasses and in crowds departed to the scene of revelry.

"Judge Bean scratched his head and called for his friend Schofield.

" 'Now look here, Schofield, it ain't in keeping with justice that all this amount of beer I have imported for this occasion should go to waste,' he said. 'It ain't economy and it ain't accordin' to the Statutes of the State of Texas.

" 'I'll pull Torres for conducting a disorderly house. There are more ways than one of doing business.' "

So Torres was arrested, his case docketed, and the date set for his trial. Meanwhile, of course, he ceased to do business and Roy's beer sales came back to somewhere near normal.

Just before the case was called for trial, Mr. Cunningham, Inspector of Customs stationed at Langtry, agreed to act as attorney for the defense. Furthermore he told Roy bluntly that he was going to appeal if the decision went against his client.

Roy told him just as bluntly that nobody ever appealed from his decisions. He didn't allow it. Nevertheless he was worried, and when next morning the case was called, his worries increased.

Mr. Cunningham was a well educated man with more than a smattering of legal knowledge. He objected to Roy's way of handling things and stumped the Judge several times by quoting the law to him.

All Roy could do was to reply doggedly, "If what you say is the law, and is in the book, and ain't a good law, then I'll tear it out of the book."

In the end the jury disagreed, thus saving Roy's judicial hide. The case was dropped for the time being, but it was by no means finished.

A year later Bean ran into Mr. Schofield on the streets of San Antonio.

"Well, I finally got the best of Torres," he said. "A jackleg lawyer turned up in Langtry broke some time ago, and in discussing the case with him, I found out that Cunningham had no right to practice law. The lawyer told me if he did not have a license he had no right to defend Torres. After that things looked easy. I called on Torres and told him that I had him. The thing I sprung on him was that I had discovered that Cunningham did not have a license to practice law, and therefore his action in defending him was illegal and contrary to the Constitution of the State and the United States, and if he wanted to plead guilty, it would cost him twenty-five dollars, but if he did not, then I would try him again and stick him to the limit. Torres came across and paid the twenty-five dollars."

With only an occasional outburst of opposition, like this move of Torres, Roy carried on his business. Mostly he sold beer and mostly it was drunk warm from the bottle. Whiskey was obtainable, and sometimes it was a home-made concoction of raw alcohol, water, cut-plug tobacco, and other mysterious ingredients. Even this awful mixture was too weak for some Texas stomachs. One story which has gone through many variations tells what happened to a son of Alkali Ike who came in and shouted, "Gimme something strong—something hot!"

Roy gave him some very special whiskey.

"Throw this rainwater out and get me something stronger," ordered the newcomer. "Gimme some real tarantula juice!"

"Oh, you want pure pizen, do you?" cracked Roy, and he reached up to a shelf behind the bar where two or three dead tarantulas bobbed gently in a jar of alcohol.

"There's your tarantula juice," he said grimly, "and by God you'll drink it!"

The cowboy took one look, turned deadly pale, and left in a hurry. At least that is one version. Another says he drank the "pizen" and died in convulsions before he could get to his horse.

Such episodes were amusing but didn't bring in much money. Usually Roy preferred to let the Alkali Ikes get drunk. In the morning he would hale them into court and fine them. Oddly enough he always seemed to know just how much a man had in his pocket and would set the fine at exactly that amount. Sometimes he miscalculated, but if he found out in time he tried, as he would have said, to "rectify the error."

One young cowboy, for instance, was brought up before the court and fined what the Judge thought he had. Mr. Cunningham was sitting by and whispered in Roy's ear, "He's got a check in his pocket."

"Then," said Roy to the cowboy, "I fine you the said amount including the check you have in your pocket."

Almost as profitable as the finable drunks were the beer and whiskey drummers who made regular stops at Langtry. It was usual for one of these men to set up drinks for everybody in the saloon whenever he made a business call. In a beer saloon the proprietor would count the empty bottles to figure up the drummer's bill, so Roy trained his helpers to keep a supply of empty bottles at hand under the bar at all times. When the drummer's back was turned these empties joined their brethren above and were counted in with the rest.

What Roy couldn't pick up by preying on drunks and drummers he extracted from that wonderful American invention, the tourist. During the last ten years of his life thousands of people visited his bar while the train stopped to take on water. Ten minutes was long enough to drink a bottle of beer, but it was never long enough for Roy to find change for a five dollar bill. Usually the passengers had to depart changeless or miss the train. When they objected, Roy handled the matter in various way. He would growl at them—threaten to handcuff them—run them off if he could. If they lost their tempers and used a damn or two, he fined them for disturbing the peace.

Now and then someone called his bluff. One tourist lost his customary calm when refused change for a dollar, picked up a beer bottle, and threatened to bash out a few Bean brains if he didn't get his money. He got his money. Another traveler with some cash coming sat down solidly as his train pulled away, announcing that he would stay right there and board it out. He and Roy thereupon became fast friends. The Judge loved a man who, like himself, was hard to bluff.

He had one favorite story on his tourist visitors. It seems that two New Yorkers got off the train one day, handkerchiefs in their breast pockets, canes over their arms, one glove off and one glove on.

They ordered beer.

Roy reached down into the straw and brought up two bottles. He uncorked them, brushed the foam off the tops with a grimy hand, and passed them over.

The tourists did not look happy. "What, no glasses?" said one.

"Ain't got no glasses here."

"This beer is hot. I can't drink it," said the other. "I can't possibly!"

"Yes, you can!" Roy snorted, and he reached under the bar for his double-barreled shotgun. "Drink your beer!"

The beer was drunk in three noble gulps apiece.

"That will be twenty dollars," said Roy.

"What! Twenty dollars for two bottles of beer?"

"No, for ten bottles apiece."

He reached under the bar again and brought out eighteen bottles. With the assistance of a roustabout he stuffed their pockets, loaded what was left into their arms, collected the money, and herded them to the train.

Naturally some of his victims tried to get back at him and sometimes they succeeded. Captain Tom Rynning in his book *Gun Notches* tells how he once acted as go-between for a friend in exchanging some sacks of barley for a couple of bottles of Roy's whiskey. There was a thin layer of bona fide barley at the top of each sack, and under that was an artful mixture of dried horse manure and gravel. When Roy found out he had been taken in, he said he "would sure as hell ventilate" Rynning next time he saw him. Rynning explained himself, however, and no trouble occurred.

That was one of the few times on record that Roy was

overreached. Most of the time he reached first and raked in the jackpot.

The last time he reached for the jackpot he was playing against the United States Government. In 1893 he filed a claim for damages sustained from Indian depredations. In his statement to the Court of Claims he said that in the summer of 1886 (he meant 1866) he was en route from San Antonio to El Paso with a train of ten twelve-mule wagons loaded with merchandise and fifteen extra mules. While he was encamped near Howard's Well, "a number of Indians belonging to the Apache tribe attacked his train and stole all the mules and the bell mare." His bill for this loss was a mere $13,500.00.

A few months before his death he told a newspaper reporter that he was in high hopes of realizing something from this claim. When he died (without leaving a will) an administrator was appointed to handle his five-thousand-dollar estate and to press the claim for Indian depredations. Nothing ever came of it and in 1910 the claim was dismissed.

The dream of easy money probably brightened the old man's last days. There wasn't much else to brighten them after Sam got into trouble

This happened in January, 1898, and might well have happened before. Sam was a quarrelsome, overbearing fellow and had scrapped around a good deal, but up to the time of the Upshaw affair he had been in no serious scrapes.

The Upshaws—mother, father, and several children—had been living at Langtry for a number of years. Mr. Upshaw, in his late fifties, was quiet and gray haired but still a husky man and not to be trifled with. He had come out to West Texas as a result of some trouble in other parts, but he was minding his own business now, avoiding difficulties, and getting on all right. His wife and children were well liked too. Sam should have picked somebody else to tangle with.

There was trouble over a Mexican blanket which Upshaw had bought. Sam thought there was something queer about the deal and developed a habit of poking fun at Upshaw whenever blankets were mentioned. Upshaw got tired of it and said he would slap Sam all over town if he didn't quit. Sam didn't quit.

One morning a party of surveyors, including Sam, came back to Langtry and rode up to the saloon. Upshaw was sitting on the gallery. He spoke to one of the men named Solon Perrin and mentioned the striped Mexican saddle blanket on Perrin's horse.

"How much did it cost you?" inquired Upshaw.

"Two and half," said Perrin.

"It's as good as the one you paid five dollars for," broke in Sam.

Upshaw sprang from the gallery where he was sitting and threw Sam to the ground. After giving him a good cuffing, he got up and walked away.

Sam ran to the door of the saloon, reached in for his old, long-barreled 45-70 rifle, knelt down, and put two bullets into Upshaw.

The wounded man stumbled a few steps and fell across the tracks.

All the men in sight disappeared at once. The only male who was willing to have seen anything was Mr. Trent, the agent at the station. He came running. So did Mrs. Dodd the storekeeper's wife, and Mrs. Upshaw.

"Sam Bean shot me twice in the back and me telling him not to," said Upshaw to his wife. Mr. Trent raised him up a little, and then life left him like a lamp going out.

It was a bad moment for everybody and was made no better by the fact that a train was due in a few minutes.

Roy Bean came over and started giving orders. He was not the justice of the peace then (Torres was), but he took charge. "Go get Torres, somebody," he barked, "and tell him to hold an inquest."

In a few minutes word was brought back that Torres refused to come. He didn't want to be the man to accuse Sam Bean of murder.

"Tell Torres to get over here quick," commanded Roy. "Tell him it will be all right, but tell him there'll be hell to pay if he don't come!"

Torres came, held the inquest, and Sam Bean was indicted for murder by the grand jury at Del Rio.

It was all but impossible to bring him off though Roy himself was willing to testify that Upshaw had a gun when he was shot. The trial was begun in September and was going badly for the Beans up to the time it was postponed—"because of illness." The story is that Sam got himself bucked off a horse and was carried to Del Rio on a stretcher. As soon as the trial had been postponed he came back and rode off on the same horse in no apparent discomfort.

Meanwhile Judge Bean and Sam were at work seeing to it that the right people did not say the wrong things. There were men within sight of the shooting who made up their minds that they were looking the other way when it happened. At least one eyewitness is said to have left the country suddenly with enough cash on hand to make up for his abandoned ranch.

Mrs. Trent, night telegraph operator and wife of the station agent, was one of the few who held their ground.

She had seen the shooting and said she had. Judge Bean
asked her husband what she was going to do about it.

"She will not say anything unless she is taken to court,"
said Mr. Trent. "Then she will tell the truth."

"Well," growled the Judge, "if Sam is sent up, he'll
get even with anybody who testified against him."

"This naturally made me nervous," says Mrs. Trent.
"Mr. Trent would stay at the office with me until eleven
or later, then he would go home. Judge Roy Bean and Sam
would come to the office heavily armed and parade
around. While my nerves were shattered, I stayed with
them."

In the end, her testimony was not taken. It was shown
that she had seen the killing through a glass window and
was therefore not a competent witness.

In the March term of court, 1899, the case was finally
heard. Sam was acquitted, but his father paid a heavy price
for the verdict. Lawyers' fees, lost business, and expenses
of other kinds had sapped his money. Worry had whitened
his gray beard. The worst blow of all fell just as he was
coming home after the trial. As the train drew up to the
station he looked out of the window at the familiar adobes
and bare yards. It was good to be coming back where he
could rest after the bad times he had gone through. Then
he noticed that there was something queer about Langtry
—something missing. A second look and he saw what was
wrong. The Jersey Lily was not there any more. It had
become a heap of charred and smoking wood. Somebody
had set fire to it while a community celebration in the
schoolhouse held the attention of all who had not gone to
Del Rio for the trial.

Roy never got over it. The good days were gone with
his home and his property. He rebuilt the Jersey Lily in

abbreviated form, played frontier judge for the boarders at Mrs. Dodd's place, and showed off at train time as usual, but the sting was gone out of him. People who made his acquaintance at this period of his life thought he was a "good, kind old man" and quite harmless. He even lost a great deal of his instinct for money making. Sometimes he grumbled when he had to leave his seat on the gallery to open a bottle of beer for a customer.

Just now and then he acted as tough as he really was. Almost the last time he appeared in print during his lifetime was in 1901. The Associated Press carried the story. A tourist had drunk a bottle of beer at the Jersey Lily and gone back to his seat in the train without paying for it. Roy noticed the oversight, decided it was due to the natural wickedness of man, and made up his mind he would do a little missionary work. Telling the conductor to hold the train, he took his old .45 and got aboard. Then he went through the cars, staring hard into every face in an effort to find the crook who had cheated him.

About half the passengers had palpitations when old Roy brought his grizzled beard and horse pistol within six inches of their noses.

Finally he found the right one and pushed his .45 into the villain's teeth.

"Thirty-five cents or I press the button," he said.

The man was scared speechless and had great difficulty in getting out a dollar bill. Roy carefully made change; then he put up his pistol and stalked out.

At the door of the car he turned and enlightened the passengers as follows:

"If you don't know what kind of hombre I am, I'll tell you. I'm the Law West of the Pecos."

BRUNO—IN MEMORIAM

It would be too bad if old Bruno couldn't have a chapter, considering how much Roy thought of him and how bad he felt when Bruno was—well, we might say murdered.

As far back as anybody can remember, Bruno was there —fat, fractious, and full grown. Other bears came and went, but it looked as if Bruno might go on indefinitely. Roy had a cage for him but never thought of asking him to stay in it. Most of the day he was attached to a corner post on the porch by a chain long enough to allow for a little circulation. The rest of the time he was fastened to a post midway between the tracks and the saloon.

He and Roy got along fine, for they had similar views on a good many of life's problems. They were both rugged souls who put up with no nonsense, and at the same time they liked to get friendly and relax with the right people. They were both acquisitive and anxious to pick up anything that came their way (the bear specialized in pullets). Both were also apt to be a bit of a shock to people who were unprepared for Beans or bears.

One day a tramp got off a freight train at Langtry and made a bee line for the well known charity of the Jersey Lily. Roy was ruminating on his porch and heard the hobo's plea.

"Go on around behind the saloon," he said, "and knock on the door. They'll give you something."

Joyfully the man skipped around the corner. Six seconds later he came tearing back in a mad scramble, eyes popping, face pale, coat missing.

"What in hell's going on here?" demanded Roy, startled out of his massive calm.

"There's a b-b-bear around there!" gibbered the frightened tramp.

A glance around the corner revealed the bear on his hind legs holding the tramp's coat and wondering what to do next. The man had run smack into him, and Bruno too was suffering from shock.

Naturally, being the Law West of the Pecos, Roy assumed the right of putting everybody else to work, and that went for Bruno. One of the bear's jobs was to assist the Judge in carrying out the mandates of the law.

It was in 1892 that a Mexican woman came to Roy for help (all the Mexicans regarded him with awe) when her husband went on a high-speed non-stop spree. Roy was sitting on his gallery with his son Sam, his constable Phil Forrest, and his friend M. W. Tracy (who tells the tale). The woman recited her sorrows with drama and pathos and Roy was much moved.

"Phil," he said, "you will find this woman's man down near Pedro's shack dead drunk. Bring him in here and look out for his knife. Sam, get that chain and lock in the back room."

In a little while Phil returned with the husband who was about as drunk and disorderly as a man might be. He could hardly hiccup an answer to the questions which were put to him. Finally Roy had him taken out and hitched by the chain to the post in front of the saloon. Then the bear was led over and padlocked to the same post, his chain being a little shorter than the one attached to the man.

Still too drunk to care about anything, the Mexican watched indifferently as the bear ambled up, drew back a paw, and slapped him into a somersault. Surprise and terror dawned upon the man's face as he rolled to the end of his chain to get out of the bear's reach. In the next half hour he sweated a week's supply of alcohol out of himself playing hide and seek with old Bruno, who was having a very happy time. When he was completely sobered up and ready to be brought before the seat of justice, Judge Bean handed down a decision. The woman was to have the family burro and household effects; the man was to have fifteen minutes to get out of town.

Roy told Tracy that the bear-and-stake method was frequently used for sobering up drunks.

That was one of Bruno's minor jobs, however. His real purpose in life was to help Roy Bean sell booze. Somehow or other he learned to like beer and became as conscientious a drinker as his master. All he asked was that somebody should loosen up the cork for him. He knew how to do everything else. He would catch a bottle that was thrown to him, get the cork out with his teeth, sit down contentedly, and tip her up. Of course people were always willing to buy a bottle of beer just to see the bear pour it down, and sometimes, along about train time, Roy would provide his pet with a free bottle so that passengers on the train would see, visit, and absorb.

Once the bear is supposed to have got drunk, broken loose, and run the Judge off into the brush, but that story is too good to be true. Bruno sometimes took offense at invasions of his personal liberty, but it was careless strangers who suffered for their rash acts. He did put a brakeman up on top of a box car one time, but he didn't mean any harm.

The brotherly relationship between Roy and his bear was really a beautiful thing, but like all beautiful things it had to end. Without realizing what he was doing Roy committed an act which made bare bones and bear skin out of Bruno.

The seed was sown when a whiskey salesman for Hugo Schmelzer dropped in for a routine call. Some say his name was Sam Betters and some say his name was something else, but Sam Betters will do. Like all the other liquor salesmen he expected to be soaked when he visited the Jersey Lily, so he bought drinks for the crowd (including Bruno), saw half a dozen empties counted slyly in with the bottles he had really bought, and prepared to pay more than he really owed. Down deep in his pocket he fished for change and brought up nothing but a twenty-dollar bill—new, crisp, and noisy. It made Roy's eyes bulge and his mouth water. He put it tenderly into his cash drawer, got a far-away look in his eyes, and seemed to forget the world around him.

The whiskey salesman finally said, "Judge, don't I get any change out of that bill?"

"The only change you got coming around here is a change of heart," said the Judge, "and by God you need it."

About that time the train whistled and the drummer went out on the run, pausing only to shake his fist at the bear who was still consuming his free bottle of suds.

A few weeks later he got his chance for revenge. Dave McCormick, who still lives in San Antonio, happened on Roy Bean in the barroom of the Menger Hotel. They coasted over to the bar and bent an elbow.

About that time the whiskey salesman came in and joined the party. They all bent elbows together.

"Where you been?" inquired Roy.

"El Paso," said the drummer.

"Did you stop in my town?"

"Sure did."

"Everything all right there?"

"Fine."

They bent elbows again.

"Oh, I forgot to tell you," said the salesman, "Bruno is dead."

"The hell you say!" Roy was deeply shocked.

"You remember you told me I could have the hide. Is your word good on that?"

"By God, you never heard of Roy Bean not making his word good, did you?"

"Well, will you sign a telegram to Sam and tell him to ship the hide to me?"

"Yes, by God!" boomed Roy. So a telegram was written out on the bar of the Menger Hotel to this effect:

Sam Bean
Langtry, Texas
   Skin Bruno and ship hide to Sam Betters at San Antonio.
                                        Roy Bean

When the telegram arrived Sam was much puzzled. He knew of no reason for sacrificing one of the family in this way, but he was an obedient son. He put two charges of buckshot between the bear's ribs and did as he was told.

Next day Roy came home and the first thing he asked was, "What did Bruno die of?"

"Of buckshot," replied Sam. "Naturally."

"You mean you killed him?" asked Roy, stunned.

"Sure."

"Why in hell did you do that?"

"I couldn't skin him alive, could I?"

That was the only time Roy's friends ever saw him mad enough to kill anybody. Fortunately he didn't see the whiskey drummer again till he had cooled off, so there was no bloodshed.

In 1896 when the big fight was run off at Langtry the bear was only a memory. A mangy mountain lion occupied the historic cage and snarled at the fight fans who looked at him.

Bears came and went around the Jersey Lily after that, but none of them could get a grip on Roy's affections. There were a couple of cubs with no personality or gumption. There was also one full-grown specimen who looked all right but soon showed signs of a nasty disposition. He clawed his chain, frightened children, and once broke the neck of a burro with a single blow of his paw. Everybody wondered what would happen if he ever got loose, and he very kindly satisfied this curiosity one day by breaking his chain and taking after his owner. The Judge dodged, ducked, and yelled for Mr. Trent, who seized his gun and solved the problem with buckshot.

After that Roy gave up trying to fill the vacant cage. Bruno had no successor.

THE BIG FIGHT

In 1896 Roy Bean's town became, for about a minute and a half, the center of the civilized world. "Langtry!" bawled the headlines in distant lands. "Langtry!" babbled excited men in Paris and London. "Langtry!" bleated every American sport between the Barbary Coast and the Bronx. From towns hundreds of miles away prominent citizens set out on pilgrimage to West Texas, and from even remoter distances came a cloud of short-card gamblers, pickpockets, pitch men, prostitutes, and phonies to bring an unusual taste of foreign culture to the Pecos country.

1896 was, in short, the year Roy Bean staged the Fitzsimmons-Maher championship fight on a sandy flat in the Rio Grande Canyon, a stone's throw from his front porch.

It was the peak of his career and showed that he had the makings of a great man in him. Coolly he stepped into the glare of world-wide publicity, pulled off the big show without a hitch, and never turned a hair of his grizzled beard.

How Bob Fitzsimmons came to knock Peter Maher loose from his doubtful world's championship that rainy February afternoon needs a little preliminary explanation. The story begins at New Orleans in 1892 when red-headed, rubbery "Fitz" licked Peter Maher, the grim champion of Ireland. Fitz immediately started gunning for Gentleman Jim Corbett and the title.

Corbett ignored the challenge as long as he could. He

was busy with his theatrical engagements and wasn't so fond of fighting anyway. He wished these unpleasant bruisers would brawl among themselves and let him alone. Fitz continued to pester him, however, and sporting citizens all over the country began yelling for the match at the top of their lungs. When he could hold out no longer, Corbett told promoter Dan Stuart to go ahead and arrange the fight. Stuart announced that Dallas, Texas, would be the place of combat.

At this time the whole United States was suffering severe pangs of conscience about its sins. Mrs. Bloomer was drawing loud cries from the pious with her indecent ideas about women's clothing. Pure and delicate-minded ladies were swooning at the sight of their misguided sisters bestriding bicycles. Any abandoned female who was suspected of smoking cigarettes in secret was cast out by society. The Demon Rum was on his knees begging for mercy. Even the manly art of boxing was taking a beating, and for a while the promoters could hardly find a place to stage a prize fight in peace.

Dan Stuart thought he might manage it in Texas, one of the few places where there was no anti-prize-fight law, but he was wrong. Governor Culberson called a special session of the Legislature and in two days made it illegal to swap punches for money in his state.

Thrown out by Texas, Dan Stuart next turned to Arkansas and arranged to put on the match at Hot Springs. But the Governor of Arkansas, like the Governor of Texas, was filled with loathing at the thought of such degraded brutality and resolved to preserve the fair fame of Arkansas from stain. When Corbett and Fitzsimmons crossed the state line, he had each one arrested for conspiracy to assault the other.

Corbett had been exchanging insults with Fitzsimmons for several months and gradually working himself up to fighting pitch, but now his temperature dropped suddenly. He announced that he would vacate the championship in favor of the winner of a projected meeting between Peter Maher and a fairly well known heavyweight named O'Donnell. This match was run off in the wilds of Nevada. Maher won. And so Dan Stuart had his preliminary build-up for a battle of the century between Fitzsimmons and Maher. Fitzsimmons was willing to beat Maher again. Maher was willing to extract the sting of a previous defeat. All that remained was to find a place where the bout could be arranged without interference.

Rumors concerning the place of battle buzzed up and down the wires past Langtry, but Roy Bean gave no sign. His hour had not yet come.

Four hundred miles to the west of him, however, a Great Idea took root. El Paso was a wide open town in those days, ten years before the inevitable cleanup. But El Paso was too far from centers of population to take the lead she deserved in sporting matters. Here was Opportunity banging on the gate. The Great Idea caught on and nearly broke up the town.

Dan Stuart was surprised when he got a proposal from the business men of El Paso offering him a six-thousand-dollar bonus if he chose their city for the contest. Then he remembered where El Paso was. Old Mexico was just across the river. New Mexico was only a few miles away, and Arizona could be reached overnight. Why not keep the location of the fight a secret till the last minute and then go wherever the coast was clear? How would Valentine's Day do for a date?

He accepted El Paso's offer. And Roy Bean kept on selling bottled beer at Langtry.

The effect on El Paso was volcanic. Nobody talked of anything but the big event. Business men began preparing for the greatest invasion since the fall of Rome. And when the notables began to drop in two months before The Day, El Paso's cup ran over.

Fitzsimmons came to town shortly after Christmas of 1895 and set up his training quarters in the little adobe village of Juarez just across the river in Mexico. He had a full-grown lion for a pet, a bicycle for exercise, and a free-and-easy manner for all the local sports. Soon his red head was a familiar sight. It was Fitz making a horseshoe at Noake's blacksmith shop; Fitz shaking hands with friends at the bull fight; Fitz in plug hat and diamonds playing the society swell. Even the ladies—or some of them—took to dropping in of an afternoon at Fitz's quarters to watch him spar and punch the bag.

Two weeks after Fitzsimmons arrived, Peter Maher got off the train, growled at reporters, and took himself off to Las Cruces, forty miles away, where he was to train.

The next arrival was Dan Stuart's secretary, who set up headquarters in the Sheldon Block.

Five days before the fight (to be exact about these historic dates it was February 9th) the promoter himself arrived, his portly frame exuding a serene confidence and his persuasive tongue casting a golden radiance over the whole future of boxing. "Nothing short of lightning or the destruction of the earth by fire or flood can stop the contests we have arranged to pull off. It is a cold 200 to 1 shot that they will come off as advertised," he said.

He announced, moreover, a magnificent scheme which

knocked everybody over with its bold simplicity. He proposed to hold a "Fistic Carnival" which would last a week,
bring thousands of people and dollars to El Paso, and make
the desert blossom with booze and bank accounts. An
arena was to be built for twenty thousand people, and
seats were to cost from ten to forty dollars. The heavyweight match was to be fought on the first day—February
14, 1896—for a purse of ten thousand dollars. On the four
days following, four other fights were to be held—three
of them for world's championships—and deals had already
been closed with the three champions who were to appear. John L. Sullivan and Paddy Ryan, with their theatrical troupe, let it be known that they would follow the
money to El Paso. Dan Stuart's office began chopping off
blocks of tickets and sending them away. Special railroad rates were arranged for. The boarding-house keepers
got out extra cots. It looked as if El Paso was about to hit
the jackpot at the foot of the rainbow.

Down at Langtry Roy Bean sat in on a poker session
and kept his mind on the game.

Less than a week before the great day! El Paso was
abuzz with bits of gossip and information.

Dixon, Walcott, Everhart, Leeds, and other principals
in the "fistic carnival" were arriving.

It was reported that Señor José de Moreno was on his
way from Madrid with six bull fighters of fabulous skill
who would thrill the audience in the mornings and whet
their appetites for the pugilistic glories of the afternoons.

A great "cowboy tournament" (forerunner of the
rodeo) set up on the outskirts of town.

Every gambler within hundreds of miles not confined
to jail or the hospital came drifting in, sniffing the prey,
while stories circulated of gambling tables in Juarez with

a hundred thousand dollars in cold cash stacked on top.

Pickpockets by the dozen began to prey on the drunk and the unwary.

Even religion came in to take its toll. Evangelist Mysonheimer, the boy preacher, with a reported score of nine thousand converts to his credit, displayed his own variety of championship form at the First Methodist Church.

Such days as these El Paso had never seen before.

But gradually a sour note began to be heard in the symphony of joy and profit. Captain Hughes, encamped with his ranger company at the near-by town of Ysleta, received instructions from Austin to look out for violators of the anti-prize-fight law. Dan Stuart was told about it, but he brushed the difficulty grandly aside. "No combination that does not involve the death of the principals," he declared, "can prevent the meeting of the men matched."

Stuart must have seen the fatal finger writing on the wall even as early as this, but he never flinched. Nobody in a tight place ever acted more at ease. At first he even disdained to reply when his enemies came out from ambush, revealed themselves as the Ministers' Union of El Paso, and began to tell the world about the brutality and indecency of prize fighting. He let his secretary answer them.

W. K. Wheelock, the secretary, made a manful defense which deserves to be rescued from oblivion. The ministers, he said, were talking about boxing twenty years ago. "The Marquis of Queensberry's rules require that five-ounce gloves be used, and this fact, along with certain rules, has taken the brutality out of the affair and made it a refined sport that could be, and is, witnessed by the most refined people. There is nothing that occurs in the present glove contests that would bring a blush to the cheek of the most refined lady in the land."

When the ministers still insisted on their point of view, Wheelock continued to emphasize the refined and delicate virtues of boxing. "I do not," said he, "make the comparison with either baseball, football, or polo, as they are so brutal and dangerous that a comparison would not be fair." Then, remembering El Paso's reputation, he added, "More physical culture and less six-shooters is my idea."

Still the ministers hammered away in sermons, in the newspapers, in appeals to the mighty of the land. They were particularly earnest with the governor of New Mexico, for they were convinced (and rightly) that Dan Stuart was scheming to hold his exhibition in that state. Governor Thornton replied that he was "powerless to prevent" the horror from taking place, though he was with them in spirit.

As a last resort the embattled ministers took the matter to Washington. They sent off a wire to Congressman Cockrell:

Undoubtedly prize fights in New Mexico, neither territorial law nor federal law prohibiting. Can't Congress prohibit immediately.

Congress could. Tom Catron of New Mexico heaved his huge bulk around and got a bill passed making it a felony to engage in any "pugilistic encounter between man and man or fight between man and bull or any other animal for money or for other things of value, or for any championship" in any of the territories of the United States.

Severe as was the blow, Stuart's superb confidence never relaxed. He said positively, "No power in heaven or on earth can stop the fights unless a national calamity intervenes."

Two days later Adjutant General Mabry arrived from Austin, bringing Ranger Captains Rogers and Brooks with ten stalwart fighting men. He said that Captain Mc-Donald of Amarillo would be along shortly and maybe some others from farther east. Dan Stuart remarked cheerfully that he had just received four hundred and twelve telegrams and seven hundred and eighty-two letters in one day.

They told him that Governor Thornton and twelve deputy United States marshals were at the Pierson conferring with the Adjutant General of Texas. Stuart launched into a discussion of the three thousand orders for seats which he had on hand.

When the news came in that the Governor of Arizona had notified the state militia to hold itself in readiness and that Governor Ahumada of the State of Chihuahua had arrived in Juarez with a hundred and fifty cavalrymen to keep the fights out of Mexico, Dan Stuart stood like the Rock of Gibraltar. He told interviewers about the Kinetoscope, miracle of the age! It would take forty pictures a minute and was charged for two hundred minutes—"an idea which could have originated only in the brain of such a man as Edison."

How Stuart kept it up is a mystery, but he did, even when Colonel Barker, commanding Fort Bliss, issued orders that no officers should leave the post after 6 P.M., just in case there should be an emergency call. Dan Stuart said with grand simplicity, "The fights positively will be held."

The public was shaken by winds of doubt. One newspaperman put the prevailing puzzlement into verse:

The Carnival

Where shall it be? Up in a balloon or on the desert bare,
On mesa or in river bed, the echoes answer "where?"
Some say it shall not be at all, but one stands undismayed
Altho the powers of heaven and earth against him are
    arrayed——
Dan Stuart says "It shall be!"

The government vows it shall not be in Texas or New
    Mexico,
And Diaz vows within his bounds the boxers dare not go.
But ministers may preach and rave and rangers scour the
    plains,
The hero of the carnival treats threats with cold disdain,
Dan Stuart says "It shall be!"

From east and west and north and south the crowds are pour-
    ing in,
For there are wise and honest men who think such fights no
    sin,
El Paso men stretch forth their hands and welcome one and
    all.
They trust the word of that cool man whom nothing can
    appall,
Dan Stuart says "It shall be!"

The only relief the harassed bystanders could find was
to attend the performances of *The Wicklow Postman* in
which John L. Sullivan and Paddy Ryan enacted a fight
scene while the better known sports then in residence
sat on the stage and represented the spectators of the
match.

It was only a matter of hours now until the gong would sound, but still Roy Bean held his peace at Langtry.

The evening of the thirteenth came and went and even yet no one knew where the fight would be held. To all uneasy inquirers Dan Stuart simply said, "Come around to headquarters tomorrow and the location of the fight will be announced." But on the morning of the fourteenth the word went out that everything had been postponed.

Why?

Well, Peter Maher had come down from Las Cruces with eyes so badly inflamed that he couldn't see across the room. Dr. White diagnosed his trouble as "acute ophthalmia" and said Peter would be well in a couple of days or maybe a week. He had got some alkali dust in his eyes and they were very sore.

Skeptics immediately began to question Maher's courage, which, by the way, had been questioned before. One newspaper dispatch said, "Sand in the eyes is a mighty poor substitute for sand in the craw."

Anyway there was nothing to do but put the meeting off. Fitzsimmons got very much excited, as usual, and raised a fuss about the thousand dollars of "appearance money" which he considered forfeit. When he had calmed down enough to think about something else, he agreed to allow Maher a week for treatment. Dan Stuart at once announced that the encounter would positively take place on Friday, the twenty-first of February.

By now a large proportion of the prospective customers had had enough. Peter Maher's eyes had wrecked the great Fistic Carnival. People who had been paying five dollars a night to sleep on a cot in somebody's hallway began leaving town. Dan Stuart called off all the lesser fights, and the disappointed boxers entrained for

other parts. He still maintained, however, that the big
bout would be fought, and such was his confidence that
many believed him.

Meanwhile the comedy went forward at a brisker
pace. On February 15th Governor Hughes of Arizona
got out the National Guard, three companies of it. The
Tucson *Citizen* was very indignant:

Of all the continental tomfoolery the territory of Arizona
has ever been guilty of it is the sending of the Arizona militia
to chase jack rabbits up and down the San Simon Valley. . . .
The idea of ordering out three or four companies of militia
to stop a couple of windy pugs from pummelling one another
is a ridiculous farce. If the brutes cross the line, let the sheriff
of the county arrest them, or better yet, let them fight if they
want to. They will not hurt one another and if they do what
difference does it make to anyone in Arizona?

And now, with no word from Stuart to quiet the curiosity raging under every vest in town, the human imagination came magnificently into play. One story had it
that the fighters were going by train to Galveston where
a steam tug would tow a barge out into the Gulf of Mexico. The fight would take place on the barge before the
Kinetoscope and a few witnesses. Eastern papers published fantastic tales about an arena "located in a spot in
the mountains where the foot of man had never before
trod and which could be held against a regiment of soldiers by a few men, as there was only a narrow pass leading to it."

At this moment Roy Bean felt the spirit move him. He
walked with great deliberation over to the railroad station and told Mr. Trent, the operator, that he wanted to
send a telegram. A few minutes later Dan Stuart was

considering an invitation to bring the prize fight to Langtry where the Law West of the Pecos would see that there
was no interference.

It did not take Stuart long to make up his mind. He
figured that the east-bound train reached Roy's town at
1:32 P.M. and the west-bound train a couple of hours
later—time enough for a boxing match before evening. In
spite of his outward calm Stuart was growing desperate.
He wired Roy an acceptance.

It was probably on Monday the seventeenth that the
arrangements were made. The El Paso papers remarked
on that date, "It is now the monthly period when different
parts of the world are sending in telegrams that they have
a spot where the fight can be pulled off without interference." A few of the wise boys heard of the decision
almost as soon as it was made, but the rumor did not reach
the public ear until Thursday, the day before the fight
took place.

Everybody naturally wondered what was going on
behind the scenes, but the rangers were in a lather of
curiosity. If the promoter outwitted them and pulled
off the match, the whole force would lose face. So they put
their heads together and worked out a course of action.
They decided to watch the Kinetoscope and the lumber
for the ring. Where these gadgets went, the fight was
sure to go.

Ranger Ed Aten and a companion were detailed to
watch the ring. They were on the job when it was loaded
onto a flat car and hitched to a west-bound freight—
destination Strauss, New Mexico, first station west of El
Paso. Aten got on the engine to accompany the lumber to
the state line.

"You're not going to ride on this engine," declared

the engineer. "If you try it, I'll knock you off with the shovel."

He was the scaredest engineer in Texas when Aten eased the muzzle of a .45 up against his stomach and told him what to do next.

The ring was actually taken to Strauss, probably to throw the officers off the scent; then it came back and went on through. The rangers spotted the car and knew something was up. Aten got aboard the first passenger train to follow the elusive flat car and found himself in the company of the carpenters who were to put up the ring.

Sure enough, the men got off at Langtry, four hundred miles east of El Paso. Before they hit the dirt, their coats were off and they were reaching for hammer and nails.

Aten went to the telegraph office to communicate with Captain Hughes. One of Roy Bean's men tried to bribe him to hold the message, but he wouldn't, and in a few minutes the rangers knew all.

Not so the public, however. About noon of the twentieth Maher came down from Las Cruces. At five o'clock Dan Stuart posted a notice on the window of his headquarters:

"Persons desirous of attending the prize fight will report at these headquarters tonight at 9:45 o'clock. Railroad fare for the round trip will not exceed $12.00."

Shortly after nine the crowd began to drift toward the depot. The pickpockets did a notable business. The railroad company did somewhat worse, but sold around three hundred tickets. Ten cars were hastily got ready to be added to the evening train, which fortunately was an hour late. A little before midnight fighters and fans headed east, accompanied by Adjutant General Mabry

and half his ranger force. The other half remained to
protect El Paso from the featherless birds of prey it had
invited in.

All night and half the next day the train chugged east-
ward. The rich boys went to bed in sleeping-car berths.
The poor ones roosted in the day coaches. Pocket pistols
(slang of the period for flasks) comforted many. But a
cold drizzle was falling long before the train reached
Langtry, and the Battle of the Century began to seem a
bit unnecessary.

Roy Bean was ready for business when at 3 P.M. the
train pulled in. All the sports piled off. Some stopped
to buy beer at a dollar a bottle at the Jersey Lily. Most
of them began scrambling down the rocky path to the
river bottom where they found a temporary bridge span-
ning the muddy waters. They crossed it—at least about
two hundred of them did—and were at the bottom of the
Rio Grande Canyon in the State of Coahuila, Mexico, beyond the jurisdiction of rangers, ministers, governors, and
legislatures.

There was the ring on a sandy flat, hedged by a canvas wall to keep non-paying guests from looking. The
non-paying guests, however, including the rangers, never
even came down from the top of the cliff. They squatted
on the rocks, two hundred feet above the arena, and saw
it all in comfort and for nothing.

At 4:15 Fitzsimmons emerged from his improvised
dressing room and climbed through the ropes; Maher
slipped in a moment later. Fitz was confident and steady;
Maher was pale.

They chose their gloves from two sets in the middle
of the ring. Julian, Fitzsimmons' manager, asked if the
prize money was at the ringside. Referee George Siler

of the Chicago *Tribune* produced two certified checks.

Julian spurned them indignantly. "I want money. These checks are no good to us!"

Fitzsimmons settled the squabble by addressing the crowd. "I am going to fight to satisfy the public, money or no money. This, however, will be the last time I will ever give under."

The crowd: "Hurrah for Fitz!"

Time now for instructions in the center of the ring—hand-shaking—the five-second whistle. Then the gong.

The men started fighting with no preliminary sparring. Fitz feinted with his right and stepped away as Maher swung; then, while Maher was off balance, Fitz landed lightly left and right on his head. Maher swung again and missed. Fitz let loose a right uppercut and missed, and they clinched. In the break-away Maher landed on Fitz's right cheek.

"Ain't that a foul?" yelled Fitz, and the referee reprimanded Maher.

Then the fists began to fly so fast the spectators could hardly see what was happening. Fitz was pushed back. He was on the ropes. Maher was landing lefts and rights which would have finished Fitz "if his head had not been on a pivot."

The crowd held its breath.

"Maher's got him," somebody groaned.

But not yet. There was another clinch. They broke in the center of the ring and Maher lashed out at Fitzsimmons' chin. Fitz got his left arm in the way of the blow. Then, as easily as if he had been polishing off a good dinner, he planted a short right hook on Maher's jaw.

Maher's head dropped. He trembled all over—then fell

heavily backwards. His head bounced off the canvas like a rubber ball, and he passed out in an ungainly position, "his head and feet slightly raised from the platform, and his eyes turned white."

It was all over in the first round after less than two minutes of fighting. The crowd broke into the ring, broke out again, and headed up the bluff for the train. A few stayed to hear a pronouncement from Maher which deserves to be remembered as a masterpiece of simple and effective narrative:

"I thought I had him licked until he punched me under the jaw and then it was all over with me and I quit thinking."

The west-bound train moved out in two sections almost as soon as the fight was over. A few more bottles over the bar and Langtry was no longer the center of the universe. Peace came once more to the Jersey Lily; and Roy Bean, counting his change, made no gesture of regret.

It was different at El Paso and Las Cruces. Several of Fitzsimmons' creditors "are now sighing for a sight of his auburn locks," said the El Paso *Herald*, and added that "calling the name of the Honorable Peter Maher in Las Cruces is like waving a red flag at a bull."

But then it always costs money to rub elbows with the great. The only person who came out ahead was apparently the proprietor of the Jersey Lily, and he was pretty close to being a great man himself.

THE JERSEY LILY

You MIGHT SAY that Roy Bean fell in love with Lily Langtry between a horse thief and a whiskey bottle. It was when Vinegaroon was at its wildest and he was dishing out law and liquor with both hands that he was smitten. A picture of her fell in his way, it is said; he took one look; and that was that.

From then on for twenty years he was her humble servant. He named his saloon and his town in her honor. He urged her by letter to drop in for a visit. He tacked her picture up on the wall of his barroom (where it gazed upon some sights that would have astonished its original). He spoke of her tenderly and often.

On her side there was considerably less emotion, but she rather enjoyed the friendship—when she happened to think of it.

They never met; but they may have seen each other five years after their acquaintance began. The interval had certainly whetted Roy's appetite for a look at those lovely features. She was now at the peak of her sensational reputation. She had toured the States for five seasons and had dazzled the eyes of thousands of American males from Hell Gate to the Hassayampa. The papers were full of her photographs. The gossip columns tattled about her friends and her foibles. She seemed more wonderful by the hour. And then, in the spring of 1888, the news came that she was to visit Texas.

She was on her way to California; maybe she would take the Southern Pacific and pass through Langtry, thought Roy. No! That couldn't be. The papers said she was to go north from San Antonio to Austin and Fort Worth. Well, maybe some other time she would travel that way. And in the meantime she was absolutely and positively to play in San Antonio. The Prince Albert coat and plug hat came out of Roy's trunk and went several rounds with a clothes brush, taking heavy punishment.

In March the papers began building up for the Lily's Texas tour. Early in April she was in New Orleans. By the middle of the month she had reached Galveston with her company and was preparing for two performances.

On the eighteenth she gave an interview in her private car to a young man from the Galveston *News*.

"Well," asked the reporter with bright originality, "what do you think of Texas?"

"This is my first visit to Texas," said Mrs. Langtry, trying hard to be charmed with the state. "I am surprised beyond measure and somewhat ashamed to confess to you the ideas I had about Texas from impressions gleaned from the newspapers at the north and east. These newspapers do Texas a great injustice. Such was my dread of the state before entering it that I thought it best to leave my jewels in New Orleans, for I had no idea of being held up by a lot of cowboys and being made to stand and deliver."

"Would you risk the cowboys now from what you have seen of them?"

"Well, I have seen no cowboys as yet, but I have seen enough to convince me that I and my possessions are quite as safe in Texas as in any state in the Union."

With these kind words Mrs. Langtry went on to Houston (where Coghlan, her leading man, had a fight with a policeman on the station platform) and to San Antonio, where she appeared on April 20 and 21.

It was a great occasion. San Antonio was in raptures over the Lily's "magnificent Juno-like beauty," her charm and intelligence, her sumptuous wardrobe.

"Farewell, oh languorous Lily," sighed the *Express* reporter who covered her performances, "a long farewell to your gowns. San Antonio has seen, admired, devoured with its eyes. San Antonio has paid. Let us hope you carry with you that satisfaction which insures a good digestion. Rest assured that we have had our money's worth."

Was Roy Bean in the audience that saw *A Wife's Peril* and *As in a Looking Glass?* Of course he was! Where else would he have been but in the front row center with his best clothes on, his beard trimmed, and the light of adoration in his foxy eye?

It was the only good chance he ever had to see her. From San Antonio she went to Austin and Fort Worth and so on to Los Angeles where she trod the boards again early in May. Roy never ceased to hope that she would come back. Close by his saloon he set up a frame building on which he put a sign reading:

ROY BEAN'S OPERA HOUSE TOWN HALL AND SEAT OF JUSTICE

Sometimes he would speak wishfully of getting Mrs. Langtry to put on a performance in her own opera house, but it was too late. A few months after her Texas tour she was back in England and did not return for years.

Hope lingered in old Roy's breast, however, and in 1903 it began to look as if his endurance might get results after all. Again the Jersey Lily was on tour and this time her itinerary would take her by way of San Antonio and El Paso—she would pass through her town at last.

Roy knew she was coming. They say at Langtry that the actress herself notified him by wire of her plans. He sent her a live wild turkey for Christmas that year and was busy with the details of a mighty reception for her when his health began to fail. He called in his friend Dodd and instructed him in the proper procedure, just in case something happened.

In March, 1903, Roy died.

Mrs. Langtry did not reach West Texas until ten months later, but plans for the reception were not allowed to drop. The Southern Pacific agreed to hold the train while the ceremonies were being conducted, and word of what was about to happen went up and down the line, eventually filtering out to the most isolated ranches.

At six in the afternoon on January 4, 1904, the Sunset Limited pulled up to the Langtry station where a large and breathless crowd was waiting. There was Mr. Dodd, Judge Bean's friend and successor, in his derby hat ready to act as master of ceremonies. There was the entire enrollment of the Langtry school, released from the classroom and drawn up in mass formation. There were cowboys and ranchers from miles away in their best hats and boots.

Eagerly they scanned the long train for a sign of their guest.

"There she is!" yelled a cowboy.

Sure enough there she was, getting down from the platform of the rear coach. Everybody rushed toward the end of the train in a great cloud of dust as Mrs. Langtry came toward them with both hands outstretched.

She was in her fifties now and no longer the ravishing creature of twenty-five years before. It was a rather plump, middle-aged woman in a flower-garden hat who started shaking hands with everybody, but to her town she was still beautiful.

When the greetings were over, the citizens fell back and a thirteen-year-old girl stepped forward with a well memorized speech just ready to pop from her lips. It was Laura Torres, daughter of Roy's old-time rival.

"Mrs. Langtry, Ladies and Gentlemen," she began. "In the name of my schoolmates and all the citizens I beg leave to address a few words of welcome to our fair English lady, the Jersey Lily. We all feel proud indeed to have the honor of greeting and shaking hands with the talented lady whose name our town bears, and who, although coming from a distant land, has taken the trouble to stop and greet the citizens of her namesake town. . . ."

And so on steadily to the end.

It was a noble effort for a shy little girl. The grown-ups were very proud and the visitor was very gracious. She handed Laura a picture of herself as a souvenir and then they all trooped over to the Jersey Lily saloon which was cleaned up, but otherwise just as Roy had left it. A deck of cards was lying on a poker table. "I'll just cut the cards for luck," said Mrs. Langtry. Then she picked up a few poker chips for remembrances and the crowd moved on to the schoolhouse, a poor little hut which had been badly damaged by a storm some years before. After looking it over sympathetically, Mrs. Langtry handed Mr. Dodd sixty dollars to "start a library" in the school (the money was used to enlarge and repair the building). Then Mr. Dodd made a little speech, presented her with Roy's old six-shooter, and it was all over but the shooting. There wasn't much of that—just a few valedictory explosions as the train pulled out.

Twenty years later the experience was still vivid in Mrs.

Langtry's mind and she described it as follows in her memoirs:

"The afternoon sun was blazing down on the parched sandy plain, with its monotonous clothing of sage-brush and low-growing cactus, when the Sunset Express came to a sudden stop. A casual glance from the window of the 'Lalee' revealed no reason why we should pause there rather than at any other point of the continuous grey desert, but the three woolly heads of my devoted 'staff' made a simultaneous appearance in the door-way of the saloon, announcing, in an excited chorus, that we were actually at Langtry, but, on account of my car being, as usual, placed at the tail end of the long train, we could see no sign of habitation.

"I hurriedly alighted, just as a cloud of sand heralded the approach of a numerous throng of citizens ploughing their way along the entire length of the train to give me the 'glad hand.' That the order of procedure had been thought out and organized was soon evident, for at the head of the ceremonious procession were the officials of the little Texas town, who received me very heartily.

"Justice of the Peace Dodd, a quiet, interesting man, introduced himself, and then presented Postmaster Fielding, Stationmaster Smith, and other persons of consequence. Next in order came a number of cowboys, who were also formally introduced. Langtry did not boast a newspaper, and therefore these young men had been gathered in from the ranges by means of mounted messengers. They were all garbed in their finest leathers and most flamboyant shirts, as became the occasion, making a picturesque group, one loosing off his gun as he passed me, in tangible proof of his appreciation of my visit.

"Thirty or forty girls, all about fifteen or sixteen, fol-

lowed, and were announced *en bloc* as 'the young ladies
of Langtry.' And, finally, 'our wives' brought up the
rear. Justice Dodd then welcomed me in an apt speech,
and, after recounting the history of the town from its in-
ception, declared that it would have been the proudest
day in the late 'King' Bean's life (he had been dead only
a few months) if he had lived to meet me, adding, with
obvious embarrassment, that his eldest son, aged twenty-
one, who had been cast for a leading rôle in this unique
reception, had received a sudden summons to San Francisco on important business. But it was generally whispered that he had taken fright at the prospect of the responsible part he was to play, and was lying in hiding
somewhere among the universal sage-brush.

"The special concession allowed by the railway authorities being limited to half an hour, I was regretfully unable
to see the town proper, which lay across the line and some
little distance from the tiny wooden shed with 'LANGTRY'
writ large upon it, and which did duty for the station, but
happily the Jersey Lily Saloon was near at hand, and we
trudged to it through the sage-brush and prickly cactus.

"I found it a roughly built wooden two-story house,
its entire front being shaded by a piazza, on which a
chained monkey gambolled, the latter (installed when the
saloon was built) bearing the name of 'The Lily' in my
honour. The interior of the 'Ritz' of Langtry consisted
of a long, narrow room, which comprised the entire
ground floor, whence a ladder staircase led to a sleeping-
loft. One side of the room was given up to a bar, naturally the most important feature of the place—while
stoutly made tables and a few benches occupied the vacant
space. The tables showed plainly that they had been severely used, for they were slashed as if with bowie-knives,

and on each was a well-thumbed deck of playing cards. It was here that Roy Bean, Justice of the Peace, and self-styled 'Law West of the Pecos River,' used to hold his court and administer justice, which, incidentally, some-times brought 'grist to the mill.' The stories I was told of his ready wit and audacity made me indeed sorry that he had not lived over my visit.

"We still had a few minutes to see the schoolhouse, which was adjacent to the saloon, but the schoolmistress had sensibly locked the door on this great holiday, so, after pledging myself to send a suitable supply of books from San Francisco, I returned to the train. The ceme-tery was pointed out to me in the distance, and the sig-nificant fact deduced that only fifteen of the citizens buried there had died natural deaths.

"One of the officials, a large, red-bearded, exuberant person, confided to a lady of my company that he deplored not having brought me a keg of fresh-made butter, also that he had a great mind to kiss me, only he didn't know how I would take it, and I thankfully add that Miss Leila Repton had the presence of mind to put a damper on his bold design.

"On nearing the train, which was becoming rather impatient, I saw the strange sight of a huge cinnamon bear careering across the line, dragging a cowboy at the end of a long chain. The 'Lalee' was decorated with a good many cages, for on my journey through the South I had acquired a jumping frog at Charleston, an alligator in Florida, a number of horned toads, and a delightingly tame prairie dog called Bob. Hence, I suppose, the correct inference was drawn that I was fond of animals, and the boys resolved to add the late Roy Bean's pet to my collection. They hoisted the unwilling animal on to the platform, and tethered him to the rail, but happily, before I had time to rid myself of this unwelcome addition without seeming discourteous, he broke away, scattering the crowd and causing some of the *vaqueros* to start shooting wildly at all angles.

"It was a short visit, but an unforgettable one. As a substitute for the runaway bear, I was presented later with Roy Bean's revolver, which hangs in a place of honour in my English home, and bears the following inscription: 'Presented by W. D. Dodd, of Langtry, Texas, to Mrs. Lillie Langtry in honour of her visit to our town. This pistol was formerly the property of Judge Roy Bean. It aided him in finding some of his famous decisions and keeping order west of the Pecos River. It also kept order in the Jersey Lily Saloon. Kindly accept this as a small token of our regards.'"

And that is as near a correct account of the Bean-Langtry affair as it is possible now to give, but people are not willing to let it go at that. In spite of Mrs. Langtry's implication that she never laid eyes on Roy Bean and in the face of the fact that she was in Texas only once during his lifetime, legends describing their encounter are universally told and believed even by old residents of Langtry. None of them saw it happen, but they "have always understood" or "have been told" that it took place.

The story usually begins with a hot box which halted her train for a few extra minutes as she was passing through Langtry. The Pullman conductor pointed Roy out to her as an interesting character she ought to meet—so they met. Roy invited her inside the saloon and announced to the petrified bar flies: "This here is Lily Langtry, the famous beauty. Hoist her up on the bar, boys, so we can all take a good look at her, and give her a bottle of beer."

When she died in 1929, West Texas newspapers stated seriously that she had once "sat on the bench beside him and helped him administer justice."

It is too bad the story isn't true. It ought to be. In a well managed world Roy Bean and the Jersey Lily should have had a rendezvous, and anybody with faith enough to believe they had one should not be forced to rub his nose in the facts.

THE LAST OF ROY BEAN

IT WAS ALMOST three o'clock of a chilly Monday morning—the sixteenth of March, 1903. The Jersey Lily was a place of silence and shadows dimly lit by a kerosene lamp turned low.

The old Judge lay on his bed in the corner by the window. His bulk made a great bulge in the quilts, for he had grown very heavy in the last few years. Here and there in the room, quiet and sad, were the friends who knew him best. There was Mr. Ellison, foremost in court sessions and poker games, draping his powerful body over Roy's old rocking chair. There was his fifteen-year-old son Roscoe jack-knifed at the foot of the bed ready to run an errand. There were Sam Bean and Dr. Ross sitting at the Judge's head and watching his feeble breathing. There too were Billy Dodd and Jesus Torres talking quietly near the door. The old feud was almost dead now; Torres had exchanged his saloon for a little store years ago and he and Judge Bean were almost friends.

"When's Sam coming?" whispered the old man without opening his eyes. He kept asking that question over and over, not realizing that Sam had been beside him for hours —had arrived half frantic the afternoon before after a furious ride.

"I'm here, Father," said Sam in a gentler voice than any there had ever heard him use.

Mr. Dodd came over and put his hand on Sam's shoulder. "I'm sure glad you got here, Sam. He ought to have some of his family with him."

"It was a hard ride," said Sam, looking at his pants stained with sweat and lather. "I'm afraid I ruined that horse I borrowed."

"He's been asking for you ever since he came down sick."

"When did you say it happened?"

"Saturday. Some of the boys found him wandering around here in the saloon acting queer. They asked him what was the matter and he couldn't talk so they got me over and we put him to bed. I telegraphed to Del Rio for Dr. Ross, and Mr. Ellison sent for you."

"He'd been to Santone for a couple of days," explained Ellison. "Said he had a good time—went to a cockfight."

"He always liked cockfights." Sam dabbed at his eyes with the back of his hand.

"Then he got to feeling bad and came on home. I saw him Saturday morning and he said he was a little easier but had a bad cold and his heart was acting up. I guess he drank more than he should have in Santone."

"Is Sam here yet?" the Judge asked again.

"I'm here, Father. Don't you hear me?" Sam was trying to keep his voice steady.

A little longer they waited. Then Dr. Ross looked intently at his patient and bent down to listen. When he straightened up again they all knew that there was no more Law West of the Pecos.

Before daylight the news had gone out over the wire and newspapers in every corner of the United States noted that Roy Bean was gone. It was too bad he couldn't have added some of those obituary notices to the stack of clippings he had been saving. "His death," said the San Antonio *Express*, "removes another of the pioneers and old Indian fighters of West Texas and a man of strict integrity and honesty. He was not polished but from beneath his rough coating there was emitted the sparkle of the gem underneath."

He would have enjoyed that.

Sam took his father's body to Del Rio the morning of his death, and two days later the dust was sprinkled on Roy Bean's coffin in the Del Rio cemetery where he lies today.

When the friends and the sons and daughters had left the dead and gone back to the living, Sam came home to Langtry. In the frowsy loneliness of the Jersey Lily he sat down to tell his uncle in New Mexico what had happened, and this is the letter he wrote:

> Langtry, Tex
> April 2 1903

My Dear Uncle Sam

Your letter came some time ago. I was very glad to hear from you but very sorry you could not see father before he died. I feel very lonely now I am still at the old place, looking after the property father left but have not fully decided yet what I will do.

You asked me to tell you about fathers death. There was not much to tell As you probably know he has been troubled with hart failure for several years at times but never serious but on friday evening before he died he was said by the people here to be appearnly well as ever. on Saturday morning he was found quite sick and in a few hours he was unconscious he grew worse all the time untill about 3 o'clock Monday morning he died.

I was 75 miles from here when father was taken sick I was out on Devils river looking after some goats he had bought. They found it hard to locate me. I did not reach home till 3 o'clock Sunday evening after a ride of 75 miles in about seven hours. I found father in a serious unconscious state, but all had been done that could be done. My Sisters from New Orleans and Brother Roy reached here monday night we buried father on Tuesday in Del Rio he had a nice funeral from Residence of Mr. Blair a great friend of his in life.

In regards to the book there is quite a little written now but it requires a great deal to finish it yet I am trying to get all the sketches I can together and try and have it writen just as soon as possible. If you can give me a few sketches or news paper cliping of his adventures they will be appreciated and I know will help the book along. I will let you hear from me from time and send you some of the books as soon as it is published. I will close now please write soon, from your

Nephew

Samuel Bean

Sam Bean's book about his father was never finished. He probably expected to add a few touches to a manuscript which the Judge had kept around the saloon for several years. Among the perennial desires of Roy's heart was the wish to see himself written up in a book, and once he even went so far as to hire an educated Del Rio Irishman to write up his life and adventures. The biographer was to be fed and provided with a few drinks while operations went forward. He made more progress with the drinks than with the biography, however, and when the job was about half done Roy had to get rid of him. Sam probably never added much to those few pages. He was better with a gun and a rope than with a pen, and

besides his time was short. In 1907 he was cut to pieces
in a barroom brawl in Del Rio. His papers were kept for
a while by his wife's relatives but have long since disappeared.

This should bring us to the end of the story of Roy
Bean, but it doesn't. They couldn't bury all of him in
the Del Rio cemetery. Around lonely campfires in the
Big Bend country—in hotel lobbies in El Paso—in Pullman
washrooms on the Southern Pacific—even in foreign coun-
tries the legends of the Law West of the Pecos still go
round.

It seems to many, and especially to some who knew him,
that the American people could find somebody better to
lionize than an old rascal like Roy Bean. Perhaps so.
Perhaps not. It is at least natural that our armchair civilization should look back with envy and regret on the
days when hardy characters like him lived by the free
use of their hands and their wits and their guns.

And this one question needs to be asked—what if Jesse
James and Billy the Kid and Roy Bean were not quite
what the public likes to think they were? We have as
much right to make our own legends as the British and
the French and the Greeks, and maybe their material was
no better at the start than ours. Maybe Ulysses had nasty
quarrels with his wife too; anyhow he stayed away from
home for twenty years. Maybe Beowulf was just another
windy old liar when he told about that fight under water.
Maybe Robin Hood wasn't so altruistic as he pretended to
be when he took advantage of unwary travelers on the
Southern Pa—pardon—the Nottingham Road. Maybe all
such heroes were of the same breed as Roy Bean. Who
knows?

SOURCES

Roy Bean covered much territory in his lifetime, and so must everyone who wishes to trace his footsteps. Several Western writers have broken the ground. Everett Lloyd's little book *Law West of the Pecos* (San Antonio, Texas, 1935 and 1942) is the best collection to date of Roy Bean anecdotes. Ruel McDaniel in another small volume called *Vinegarroon* (Kingsport, Tenn., 1936) has done an interesting job of dramatizing the better known episodes in the Bean saga. Major Horace Bell's two books, *Reminiscences of a Ranger* (Santa Barbara, 1927) and *On the Old West Coast* (New York, 1930), give the only full account of Roy's adventures in California. The following books are also quoted in these pages:

George C. Anderson, *History of New Mexico*. Los Angeles, 1907.

Hubert Howe Bancroft, *The History of California*, vol. vi, *Works*, vol. xxiii. San Francisco, 1888.

Walter Noble Burns, *The Robin Hood of El Dorado*. New York, 1932.

F. H. Bushick, *Glamorous Days*. San Antonio, 1934.

Frederick C. Chabot, *With the Makers of San Antonio*. San Antonio, 1937.

Glenn C. Clift, *History of Maysville and Mason County*. Lexington, Kentucky, 1936.

Vinton Lee James, *Frontier and Pioneer Recollections of Early Days in San Antonio and West Texas*. Artes Graficas, San Antonio, 1938.

Lillie Langtry, *The Days I Knew*. New York, 1925.

W. W. Mills, *Forty Years at El Paso, 1858–1892*. Copyright 1901 by W. W. Mills.

Carlysle Graham Raht, *The Romance of the Davis Mountains and the Big Bend Country*. El Paso, Texas, 1919.

August Santleben, *A Texas Pioneer*. New York, 1910.

William E. Smythe, *History of San Diego*. San Diego, California, 1908.

Myron W. Tracy, "Roy Bean: Law West of the Pecos," in *Straight Texas* (Publications of the Texas Folk-Lore Society number xiii). Austin, Texas, 1937.

Old newspaper files are gold mines for anyone who wants to know about the West of yesterday. Brief mentions and extended articles on the Law West of the Pecos are to be found in the San Antonio *Express* and *Light*, the Austin *Statesman*, the El Paso *Daily Times*, *Daily Herald*, and *Lone Star*, the *Rio Grande Republican*, the Houston *Chronicle*, the Dallas *Morning News*, the San Diego *Herald*, the *Frontier Times*, the *Texaco Star*. Two useful newspaper articles are "The Halcyon Days of Vinegaroon," by Charles Merritt Barnes (*Express* for August 20 and 27, 1905) and "Forgotten Beanville," by Franklin Hall (*Express* for December 31, 1933).

Much information has turned up in various official repositories, especially in the county records of Pecos, Bexar, and Val Verde Counties in Texas and San Diego County, California; also in the records of the War Department, the United States Court of Claims, the Department of the Interior, the Post Office Department, the Bureau of the Census, and the National Archives.

Many persons have turned over the keys of their storehouses—especially Mrs. M. B. Clark of El Paso, granddaughter of Roy Bean's brother Sam; Edward S. Sears and C. Stanley Banks of San Antonio, who know their Beanville; Harriet Smither, Archivist of the Texas State Library; Mrs. Maude

D. Sullivan and Miss Edith McCright, Librarians, and the fine staff of the El Paso Public Library.

To these names should be added those of Lanier Bartlett, editor of Major Bell's reminiscences; Mrs. G. W. Hook of Holton, Indiana; Mrs. Henry Stoes of Las Cruces, New Mexico; John W. Gilcrease of Columbus, New Mexico; Mr. and Mrs. Guy Skiles of Langtry; Col. Launcelot M. Purcell of San Gabriel; W. H. Burges, Maury Kemp, Billy Wilson, and Mrs. W. D. Greet of El Paso; Helen Dorman, Librarian of the New Mexico Historical Society; Paul M. Angle, Librarian of the Illinois State Historical Society; John Davidson, Curator of the San Diego Historical Society; Mrs. Randolph Kinney of the Fort Worth Public Library; E. R. Dabney and Winnie Allen, Newspaper Curator and Archivist, respectively, at the University of Texas; Grace Arlington Owen of the San Diego Public Library; Althea Warren of the Los Angeles Public Library; Glenn C. Clift, Librarian of the Lexington Public Library; Robert Rea, Librarian of the San Francisco Public Library; Mabel R. Gillis, California State Librarian; Allie Welsh of the San Antonio Public Library.

Finally it is a pleasure to acknowledge the great debt this book owes to the men and women who knew Roy Bean and have been willing to share their memories—especially H. L. Howell, Ed Aten, R. R. Ellison, and the late Joseph L. Dwyer of El Paso; Mrs. W. H. Dodd and Harold Dodd of Langtry; Ambrose Burdwell, J. H. King, Mrs. J. H. Wallen, and Emer Billings of Del Rio; David R. McCormick, G. W. McMullen, and Mr. and Mrs. Simon Shaw of San Antonio; M. W. Tracy of Palm Beach; Mrs. R. B. Trent of Hot Springs, New Mexico; Lee Reagan of Tucson; Judge O. W. Williams of Fort Stockton, Texas; W. J. Jones of Reserve, New Mexico.

MUCHAS GRACIAS